How To Books

Planning Your
Gap Year

GW00507900

Planning Your
Gap Year

Have the time of your life working,
studying or travelling

MARK HEMPSHELL
2nd edition

How To Books

Published by How To Books Ltd,
3 Newtec Place, Magdalen Road,
Oxford OX4 1RE. United Kingdom.
Tel: (01865) 793806. Fax: (01865) 248780.
email: info@howtobooks.co.uk
http://www.howtobooks.co.uk

First published 1997
Reprinted with amendments 1999

British Library Cataloguing in Publication Data.
A catalogue record for this book is available from
the British Library.

Cover design by Shireen Nathoo Design
Cover image PhotoDisc
Cartoons by Mike Flanagan

Produced for How To Books by Deer Park Productions
Typeset by Concept Communications Ltd, Crayford, Kent
Printed and bound by Cromwell Press, Trowbridge, Wiltshire

NOTE: The material contained in this book is set out in good
faith for general guidance and no liability can be accepted
for loss or expense incurred as a result of relying in particular
circumstances on statements made in the book. Laws and
regulations are complex and liable to change, and readers should
check the current position with the relevant authorities before
making personal arrangements.

Contents

List of Illustrations

Preface

A gap year is a once-in-a-lifetime opportunity. A gap year can be *your* year, to do what you want, free from the restrictions and pressures of school, college or home. There is nothing to compare with it and it's an opportunity that almost certainly will never knock again.

Bearing this in mind you will see the need to plan your gap year very well indeed, to make the most of the opportunities you have. A badly planned gap year can so easily become a year of missed opportunities and dead end jobs, which actually makes it harder to survive at college. But with careful planning it can mean travel, adventure, new experiences, new friends, extra money to spend and a head start once you go back to full time education.

The purpose of this book is to give you inside information on some of the exciting possibilities, help you choose what's right for you and put them together into a gap year that you'll never forget.

So get planning now and start looking forward to an incredible gap year!

Mark Hempshell

1
Planning Your Year

MAKING THE DECISION TO GO

Is a gap year for you?

Before even starting to plan your gap year, think long and hard about whether it really is for *you*.

Deciding whether to take a gap year must be your decision and yours alone. It's easy to get carried along in the swing of things, according to whether your friends at school are also thinking of gap years, but really only you can decide.

The reason is simple, gap years tend to be individual affairs. It's very unlikely that two people will want exactly the same from a gap year. It's hard to take a gap year as a group, if only for practical reasons.

Some important points to consider

● A year is a very long time! In fact, a gap year is even longer: from June of one year to September the next. Whilst a long holiday might be very welcome after exams in June you also need to consider what you are going to do through the long, cold days of winter.

● Your gap year will put you a 'year behind' everyone else. Does that bother you?

● Will your course still be available a year on, and will you still be able to get a place on it then?

● Will you be able to pick up the study habit and go on, after a year working/travelling/earning real money?

● Can you afford to take a gap year, from a financial point of view? Or looked at another way, can you afford *not* to?

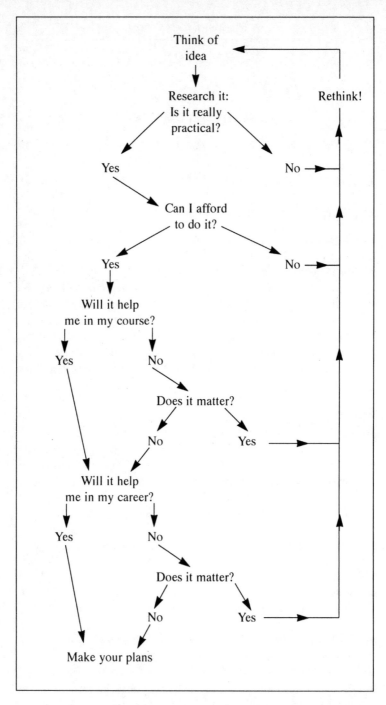

Fig. 1. Thinking through your gap year.

● If there is something you really want to do, such as travelling or voluntary work, when else will you get the chance to do it, if not now?

You may be able to think of other considerations, of course. Whatever they are, consider how much they matter to you personally.

DECIDING WHAT TO DO

A gap year offers a wide range of wonderful – and also potentially quite weird – opportunities! If anything, the difficulty will be in deciding what you won't be able to do, rather than what you will.

Having a timetable

There is, of course, nothing to say that you have to have a rigid timetable, but it will help you get the most from your time and make your gap year more productive. One point that many gap year students make is that if you don't plan it is very easy to get stuck in a rut of late mornings in bed, and even later nights, and only realise that you have wasted your time the following January, by which time half your gap year is over.

Spending time working

There are also, of course, no rights or wrongs about what you can do. There are, however, several activities that have become so popular with gap year students that it would be foolish not to give them a close look. One of these is to spend some time working.

Pros

Even if you've had a part time or weekend job for a couple of years, experience of the 'real' world of work will be an eye-opener. In fact, if it is carefully chosen you'll probably enjoy it and it can help you with your course. The money will also be very handy of course, and you might be able to save something towards your time at college.

Cons

Work can be hard to get. You might only be able to find menial jobs if you have no relevant qualifications, and this probably won't help either your bank balance or your course. Alternatively you might find you like it so much you don't want to go back to student poverty next year.

Working abroad

Pros

Working abroad offers a chance to really enjoy a foreign country much more than you can as a tourist. Working as you go is also a very good way to pay for an extended holiday. You will certainly develop your personality and may also learn new skills, such as languages.

Cons

Opportunities to work abroad are fairly limited, especially if you don't speak the langauge, and there is always lots of competition for holiday jobs. Once you take off living costs you probably won't make much money from foreign work.

Doing some voluntary work

Pros

Voluntary work can be very rewarding. It is a chance to help others whilst finding out a great deal about yourself, too. Also there are chances to do things you just can't do in the world of 'proper' work. You can even do voluntary work abroad and visit countries to which it is otherwise difficult to travel.

Cons

As the name suggests voluntary work probably won't be paid (although it is occasionally). It may even cost you money, if you want to take part in an organised programme.

Taking part in an exchange

Pros

An exchange is an ideal way to experience another way of life and another country, with support from local people. Again, exchanges can be character-building and offer a chance to learn new skills, especially languages.

Cons

Organised exchange programmes may cost money and, in fact, can be quite expensive. If you dislike your exchange and your exchange partner it can become quite an unpleasant experience.

Studying for a while

Pros

A gap year can offer a chance to add to your qualifications, away from the pressure of school or college, and to add to your range of skills and personality. Plus it allows you to keep your hand in with academic work.

Cons

After A levels more study might be just too much! It may be difficult to apply yourself, especially if the study does not lead naturally into your college course. It may cost you money, too.

Tailoring your ideas to fit

All these opportunities will be discussed in greater detail later in the book. Of course, there is nothing to say you have to stick to just one, or any, of these for your entire gap year. You can mix and match as much as you like, and also introduce your own ideas.

HOW TO MAKE THE MOST OF YOUR TIME

The best way to make the best of your time is to put together some sort of **itinerary**.

1.   Work out how much time you have.

2.   Work out what activities you want to do.

3.   Place them in order of priority.

4.   Find out realistically how much time each activity will take.

5.   Allocate time to 'must do' events.

6.   Fit your other chosen events around them.

From this basic information you can start to put together a basic itinerary. Of course, you can change it as you go along but it will help you decide which activities to look more closely at, and when and where you might fit them into your year.

The gap year planner at the end of this book (page 102) will also help you to make the most of your year.

WHAT ABOUT NEXT YEAR?

The whole purpose of a gap year is, of course, that it is a year between school and college. It assumes that you will be going back into full time education next year.

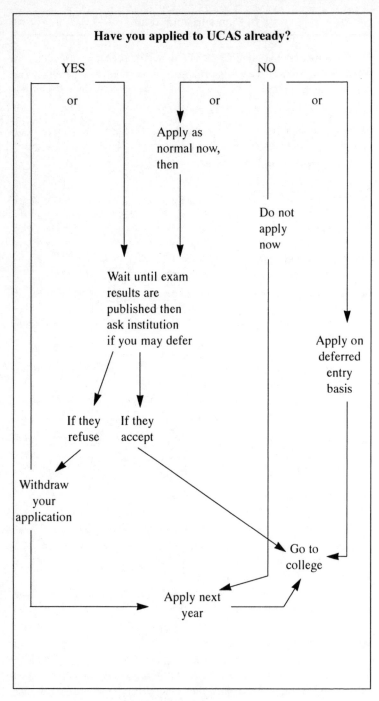

Fig. 2. Applying for your college place.

The vast majority of students who take a gap year *do* go back into education. There are no official figures, but it is thought that only about five per cent of students who take a gap year later change their minds and don't go back to college.

With this in mind you must think ahead to the year after *now*. If you have already decided what course you want to study, then that is half the battle won. If you aren't really sure about what you want to do then sort this out now. Most students agree that taking a gap year won't magically help you decide what course you want to study! It is also generally much easier to choose a course of study now, whilst you are still at school or college, than when you are away from it.

There are three way of approaching the year after:

● Apply for your course this year, then ask to change it.

● Apply for your course this year, using the **deferred entry** system.

● Do not apply now, but wait until next year.

Changing your college place

A number of gap year students apply for their college place in their last year at school, in the normal way. Then once a place has been secured they ask to change it. This is certainly *not* an officially approved method of securing your place, but universities are used to it to some degree. It may be particularly suitable if you have decided to take a gap year at the last moment.

You can ask to change your year of entry at any time after you have been offered a place. However, many students say that the best time to do this is when the A level results are published. This way universities with a shortage of places may be more willing to agree to your request. If they don't, of course, you will lose your place, have to reapply, and may not be considered for the same course because of this.

Deferring your college place

As you may already know the UCAS application system has a built-in facility if you wish to defer your college place. All you need to do, to make an application for a place the year after next, is to tick the relevant box on your UCAS form.

If you make a deferred application then note that you will be *expected* to give your reasons for wishing to defer entry in the further information section, as well as your other reasons for wishing to take the course.

Do remember that just because a box is provided on the form for deferred entry it does not mean you have any right to defer, that the institution is happy to consider deferred entries, or even that the course will exist the year after next. You will have to do your own homework here and find out whether a deferred application is likely to be successful.

Delaying your application

The third way of organising your college course for the year after your gap year is to wait until next year and then apply. That is, you apply at the same time as those applicants who are a year younger.

This is a perfectly acceptable method and alternative to deferred applications, assuming your course will still be available. However, it may or may not be suitable for you. It works best for those who are confident about:

● the course they wish to study

● getting the grades they require for it.

If you aren't so sure then it could very easily lead you into a dead end.

Also remember that it is more difficult to organise and make an application when you have left school, especially if you intend to be away from home during your gap year.

Choosing which approach to take

None of these methods is necessarily right or wrong. It is a matter of choosing the method that is best for you.

As circumstances vary from person to person, do take advice from your teachers before reaching a final decision.

Also remember that the UCAS procedure and its timetable varies slightly from year to year. Full details are given in the UCAS Handbook which is published every June for entry the following year.

You can also make general enquiries on the admissions system to the Universities and Colleges Admissions Service on (01242) 227788.

ASSESSING WHAT UNIVERSITIES AND EMPLOYERS THINK

What do universities think?

The attitude of individual universities, and individual **admissions**

tutors, towards the gap year varies considerably. Some are in favour, some have their doubts to a lesser or greater degree.

If you are to impress an admissions tutor with your gap year plans you should be able to make a case that it will be a year well spent. Working is an acceptable activity, but it is better if you can show that you will learn something from it. Travelling is acceptable, but it will impress more if your travel is other than just a holiday.

Always try to find out what the attitude is of the individual institutions you wish to apply to, and then play it by ear. You can do this at an open day, or often by phoning the admissions tutor and asking.

Finally, remember that even where the admissions tutor approves of your plans a deferred entry makes it more difficult for them to juggle the figures and balance their budget. This will always put you at a slight disadvantage.

What do employers think?

The opinions of future employers should always come second to those of universities and colleges. Employers usually approve of gap year experiences, although some are indifferent to them.

If you are hoping that your gap year will make a good impression on employers, then it should be something relevant to your career. So, for example, if you wish to work in banking a job in a bank might impress. Anything that leads to another qualification, such as a language course, is also popular with employers. Travel is less likely to impress – and some employers may even be rather sceptical about this – so if you intend to travel try to combine it with something else too.

How a gap year can enhance your CV

There is little doubt about it: *a gap year will definitely enhance your CV.*

This is particularly useful, of course, as until now you may have very little to put on your CV.

To make your gap year as CV-enhancing as possible, then, it is important not only to make the right choices but to present them on your CV in the right way:

● Balance less productive activities, such as holidays and casual work, with productive activities such as courses or study.

● Say why you chose each activity.

- Say what you did and, particularly, what you learned from it.

- Support your experiences with certificates and references where possible.

TEN THINGS TO DO BEFORE YOU LEAVE

1. Re-confirm your college place and double-check on start dates.

2. If you will be away at exam results time arrange for someone to collect or forward them for you.

3. Get an emergency contact number for your school, in case you need to discuss a last minute change of plan with them.

4. Get an emergency contact number for your intended university, in case you need to discuss a last minute change of plan with them.

5. Give notice to your employer if you have a part time job. (You might be able to get your job back when you return, or in the university vacations.)

6. If travelling, arrange for someone at home to deal with any urgent matters or emergencies for you.

7. Book your tickets for journeys where it is cheaper to book well ahead.

8. Confirm flight/train/bus departure times in case they have changed.

9. If taking up a job/course/exchange, etc, telephone just before leaving to confirm arrival dates and meeting arrangements.

10. Always have contingency plans in case things go wrong, *ie* alternative gap year activities and another choice of course for next year.

DO'S AND DON'TS

- Do think about your gap year very carefully.

- Don't do it just because everyone else is doing it, and *vice versa*.

● Don't try to plan it with anyone else.

● Do try to fit in several different activities.

● Do have your course more or less chosen before you go ahead with planning a gap year.

● Don't change plans about your course without very careful consideration.

● Don't use a gap year as an excuse because you are undecided about your future.

● Do have second choices available in case things go wrong.

● Do allow for a holiday somewhere within your gap year. This supports the idea that a gap year isn't an extended holiday.

● Do have a realistic idea of the activities you are likely to be able to do.

CASE HISTORIES

Paul goes backpacking to gain experience
Paul and two friends decided to backpack around Scandinavia in summer.

'We didn't want to follow the usual backpackers' trails so we decided to head for Denmark, Sweden and Finland,' says Paul.

'People say that Scandinavia is expensive, and it does live up to its reputation but if you spend carefully it can be done. Hotels were completely out, even the cheap ones. We used quite a few youth hostels and found private rooms fairly affordable. Food is fairly costly, too. Buying Inter Rail passes made our trip affordable and apart from that we spent hardly anything on transport.

'Copenhagen is great in summer, and it was worth the trip up into the Arctic Circle just so we can say that we've been!'

Fiona recommends good planning when she goes Greek
Fiona and a friend spent three weeks island hopping around the Greek isles in July and August.

'Island hopping is as good as they say. We're both glad that we decided to go. Once you get to Athens there's a vast choice of islands with tempting names you can choose from. It's still fairly cheap to get there and to stay once you arrive, although the touristy ones are more expensive than the others. We enjoyed a bit of everything – sun, sand, beaches, and some culture too!

'My advice to anyone thinking of doing the same would be to plan before you go. We didn't plan which, looking back, wasn't a good idea, because we only just made it back to Athens at the end of the stay.

'By the way, don't expect the ferries to fit in with your plans. They run to a laid back, we'll-get-there-when-we-get-there Greek timetable which can be maddening at times.'

Jane opts for au pairing

Jane from Wetherby decided to work as an au pair in New Jersey, USA.

'My desire to become an au pair certainly didn't have anything to do with liking children', she says. 'For quite a while I'd wanted to work and travel in the USA. But, of course, it is almost impossible to get a work visa, plus at 18 I didn't feel too confident about travelling around a foreign country by myself.

'Au pairing seemed to offer the ideal solution. Of course it wasn't just an excuse. I've always liked kids, although I don't want any of my own just yet, and done quite a bit of babysitting. If you do feel happy around children then this part of au pairing doesn't really seem like work at all.

'After looking at the various opportunities I settled on the Au Pair in America programme. Their literature is very comprehensive, but apart from promoting the exciting experiences that au pairing can offer it also stresses the responsibilities.

'My best advice to anybody thinking about au pairing is to make a list of the pros – such as the chance to travel – and the cons – such as the fact you will be away for a long period. Then sit down and balance one against the other so that you can be quite sure this is the right decision for you.'

John finds rewarding work

John spent his time as a support worker for a charity. This is what he said about it during his year.

'I work for a charity which runs several homes for the mentally handicapped. They're not great, rambling institutions, but small places that are as much like a real home as possible.

'Support worker is the right name, because I'm here to support our clients, not look after them. Support work is all about finding out what they want to do and helping them to achieve it. So, for example, if a client wants to go shopping it would be the easiest thing in the world to go out and do it for them. We don't do that. Instead we make sure that they know what to do, and where to go and then leave them to it as much as possible so they can be as independent as possible.

'Of course, it's a very rewarding job and we get a lot of affection from our clients. They see us more as friends really. This isn't a residential position, but I'm required to sleep in once or twice a week which all goes to make it more of a vocation than just a job.'

Stewart finds disadvantages in going for the money

Stewart decided he was going to use his gap year to make some decent money, and have a lot of fun too.

'As soon as I finished my last A level I went and got a job,' he says. 'I registered with a temping agency and did order picking work in a factory for the summer. It was boring, but I managed to save about £500 which I spent on a holiday in Ibiza at the end of September.

'I came back from that and got a job with WH Smith until Christmas. I saved some of what I earned there, but spent the rest on two weeks skiing.

'When I came back from Austria I got another job in a shop, and then on a farm until August, went away for another two-week holiday and then came back to get ready for university.

'All in all, I had paid for everything, had three good holidays and saved about £2,500 towards my first year at college.

'The year off taught me a lot about myself but it hasn't added anything to my CV, which I now think is a disadvantage. If I could take a year off again I would definitely take a course or some sort of organised gap year programme – something that I could use to my advantage in the future.'

CHECKLIST

1.   Is a gap year really for you?

2.   What activities would you *like* to do?

3.   Are there any activities that you *need* to do?

4.   How will a gap year affect your course?

5.   What is the best way to postpone your course?

2
Paying for Your Year

PLANNING YOUR FINANCES

What is it likely to cost?

Like any period of your life a gap year needs to be planned from a financial point of view as much as any other. In fact, it needs to be planned extremely carefully. A gap year can be an uncertain period in money terms. At some periods you may have little or no money coming in, whereas at other times you could be earning a reasonable wage. At some times you may have few expenses, whereas at other times you might have a lot of expenditure.

The general feeling is that it actually *costs money* to take a gap year. Unless you spend a lot of your time in quite a well paid job – which very few gap year students can actually manage to get – you won't be able to cover all your expenses and have a lot of money left over too. In fact, you will be quite fortunate to break even.

Here are some examples of the likely costs of different types of gap year:

- £10,000 to spend a year studying Japanese in Japan.

- £2,500 to spend time on an expedition to South America.

- £1,500 to spend the summer inter-railing round Europe.

- £800 to spend a year as an au pair.

- £400 to spend the summer on a work camp in Europe.

- Nothing to spend your year working in a shop/factory at home.

Financial planning tips

The best way to plan your finances is to reconcile your income and outgoings:

● What savings do you have, if any?

● Could you solicit any contributions from friends and relatives?

● What money could you borrow, assuming you can pay it back?

● What money are you realistically likely to be able to earn?

● Are any grants available to you?

● What will your living expenses be?

● What will travel costs be?

● Will you also be taking a holiday during your year?

● What will you have to pay for: *eg* courses, voluntary work projects, exchange programme fees?

Financial planning chart

The following chart will help you work out some likely figures.

	Highest likely	**Lowest likely**
Incomings		
Savings	_____	_____
Contributions	_____	_____
Borrowings	_____	_____
Earnings	_____	_____
Grants	_____	_____
Outgoings		
Living expenses	_____	_____
Travel	_____	_____
Holidays/entertainment	_____	_____
Fees	_____	_____
TOTAL	_____	_____

Actual figures are likely to be somewhere in the middle, but this chart will help you work out an approximate figure.

RAISING THE MONEY BY SAVING

Save as much money as possible towards your gap year as soon as you have decided to take it. It will be much easier to save now than when you are actually on your gap year.

Try to start saving as early as possible during your last year at school, well before exam pressure starts to mount.

If you can, get a part time job as soon as possible.

Budgeting for saving

Try to save to a weekly budget. Even if it is only £10 a week that's £500 over the course of year, plus a little interest on top!

Put your savings into a tax-free savings plan or apply to have the interest paid without deduction of tax, assuming you are a non-tax payer.

BORROWING FOR YOUR GAP YEAR

You may not think it is a good idea to borrow to take a gap year and, in general terms, it is not. However, there are some situations where it can make sense. For example, if you plan to travel at the start of your gap year and then get a job to pay it back, it could just be a possibility.

First look at 'unofficial' forms of borrowing, which are generally much cheaper. Could you borrow from your parents or relatives? If you are lucky you might even be able to negotiate a loan that you won't have to pay back, in full or at all!

Borrowing from commercial lenders

Commercial borrowing, using either a bank personal loan or a credit card, is a possibility only if you plan very carefully indeed. Commercial lenders will consider applications if you are in a position to pay the loan back. In this case don't underestimate how difficult it will be to get a job to pay back your loan and don't overestimate what you are likely to earn.

Given the difficulty of making both ends meet at university in any case, you don't want to start your new course with debts left over from your gap year in any circumstances.

RAISING SPONSORSHIP

If you are determined and imaginative it may be possible to get someone else to pay for part or even all of your gap year, by seeking **sponsorship** for it!

This type of arrangement is quite possible, although it is by no means easy to secure. Many companies, for example, know there can be advertising benefits for them in the right kind of sponsorship, or have a strong sense of social responsibility. Some are even actively looking for projects to sponsor and can't find enough.

You should accept that you're unlikely to be given a blank cheque to finance your gap year. Then again, if you can get a few pounds or even some practical help from a few companies it could make all the difference. One gap year student we know of secured £1,000 from a local company for a round-the-world trip, after arranging to write progress reports bearing the sponsor's name for the local newspaper. Another student secured a free flight to her voluntary work project simply by making out a good case to the airline.

Tips for raising sponsorship

- First you need to think of an **activity** that a company will want to sponsor. Ideally it should be something that will be as beneficial as possible to *them*. If it is something that will get them good publicity, so much the better.

- Structure it in such a way that the **benefits** are clear, as in the case of the world trip arrangement above.

- Think about **who** will want to sponsor you. This will probably be a company, possibly a local one. It could, however, be a charity or other organisation. Do some research and locate such organisations.

- Put a **proposal** direct to them. A letter is the best way. Don't make this look too like a circular or a begging letter and be sure to push the benefits.

- An alternative way to find sponsors is to get the **media** to cover your campaign for sponsorship. Local newspapers, radio and TV stations are often interested in this type of thing so give them a call. Get a photograph and a contact number in there too.

Claiming grants and scholarships

The chances of being able to claim a grant or sponsorship to finance, or partly finance, a gap year are fairly slim. However, it may be an option worth looking into. It very much depends on what you want to do and what the benefits will be.

If you're travelling or working there's little chance of a grant being available. However, if you are doing voluntary work, an exchange, work experience or studying then there may be possibilities.

To find out if you could be eligible for any form of grant or scholarship check with *The Educational Grants Directory* (Directory of Social Change Publication). It lists what is available in terms of educational visits and exchanges, scholarships and company sponsorships. It should be available in your local library.

EARNING YOUR WAY

Earning your way is probably the best way to fund a gap year. This doesn't mean it will all be hard work, in fact working your way can be enjoyable. You can, if you wish, plan your schedule so that you do not have to work all the time, but can simply spend a while working to pay for the next leg of your gap year.

Finding work

If you are considering this option then do remember that it can be more difficult to find work than you might expect. You might not earn very much, especially with no relevant skills and qualifications. If you wish to work abroad the situation can be even more difficult.

If you take this option then it may be a good idea to start a job as soon as possible – before all the suitable jobs are taken by students who are already at university. There are also more jobs available in the pre-Christmas rush, but a shortage in January.

If possible, try to look for a job that will benefit your future course or career, although this may not always be easy.

Claiming a tax rebate

If you have been working and paying income tax up until you take a gap year, you *may* be able to claim a **tax rebate** which will help pay for it. This is by no means certain, as it will depend on your individual circumstances, but it is worth checking out.

A tax rebate may be possible if you have had income tax deducted from your earnings (including any interest on savings), but your total earnings are below the annual **personal income tax allowance** for the current tax year.

To find out if a rebate may be possible first ask your employer for details of your pay to date and what (if any) tax had been deducted. Also ask them for details of your tax office, which will be your employer's rather than your own local office.

The relevant tax office will be able to tell you if you can make a claim.

Claiming state benefits

Unless you are registered as unemployed and claiming the appropriate benefits – which hardly qualifies as a gap year – you cannot generally claim any state benefits on a gap year, even if you do not have any other source of income.

The main exception to this is if you are undertaking voluntary work. In these cases you can do your voluntary work and, as long as you do not earn more than a nominal amount per day, you may still be entitled to state benefits as long as you remain available for full time work.

As individual cases vary so much be sure to make enquiries with your local DSS office.

CASE HISTORY

Liz and Vikky finance their gap year

Liz and Vikky explain how they raised the money for their gap year.

'Early on in the last year of our A levels we both decided that we wanted to do something really useful with our gap years. We decided that we wanted to travel for several months in the USA during the summer at the end of our gap year, and worked out that we would ideally need at least £4,000 each to pay for our trip. We knew that we wouldn't be allowed to work in the USA during our trip, so we would need all this money up front.

'We paid for our gap years through an assortment of odd jobs: part time, temporary and casual. We also asked our families for contributions instead of Christmas and birthday presents which helped swell the fund. One of our more unusual money-raising methods was to buy old photographs and postcards cheaply at car boot sales and from junk shops, frame them nicely and then sell them as 'photo antiques' at posh collectors' fairs. It worked quite well.

'We have both decided that our gap year was a very worthwhile experience. As well as travelling extensively we are both now experts at managing our money – an essential skill for all students – and we feel we are much better communicators than we ever were before.'

CHECKLIST

1. Estimate a likely cost.

2. Work out how much money you have already.

3. Work out how much money you need.

4. What is the best way to make up the difference?

3
Travel Opportunities

SPENDING SOME TIME TRAVELLING

Travel is one of the great golden opportunities for a gap year. You're unlikely ever to have so much time to go travelling again. Once at college you might not be able to afford it, and once in the world of work you probably won't be able to find the time.

Your travel might be short, or it might be long. It might be just within your own country, a single continent, or you could even go right around the world!

If you wish to travel then planning some sort of **itinerary** is essential. It may seem tempting just to take off and go where the fancy takes you, but this is a recipe for seeing a fairly small number of places, and at a high cost too. It is much better to have some idea of a route before you set off. It will save time and be cheaper. This is not to say you can't change your itinerary en route – in fact some of the best fun is to be had this way – but you should have an overall route in mind.

Where could you travel?

The world is a big place and, unless you have the resources to jet around it by air, travel is still a time consuming business. A trip around the world by surface transport in as little as 80 days is no more realistic nowadays that it was in the days of Jules Verne!

Put your priorities in order. Here are some points to bear in mind:

- What do you like? Are you interested in history, culture, general sightseeing or just having a good time?

- How much time do you have? Are you going to spend your entire year travelling, or just a few months or weeks?

- How much money do you have? Even budget travel costs money.

31

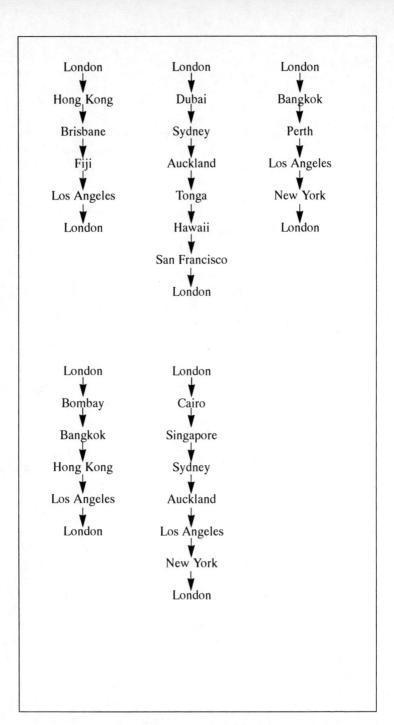

Fig. 3. Some popular round-the-world itineraries.

If you are on a really tight budget it might be better to stick to one or two countries than try to do everything.

● What time of the year will you travel? Remember that the weather in Europe and the USA does not always make for easy or pleasant travel in the winter, whereas in the summer you can go more or less anywhere.

What would you like to see?

It can be unrealistic to aim to go everywhere and see everything, even on a year-long, round-the-world trip. For example, if you go to Australia for a couple of months you'll be very hard pressed to do everything, and even then you'll want to spend more time stopping off on the way there and the way back. It is a good idea to have a sort of theme for your trip, to make the most efficient use of your time.

Try to plan your trip around those activities that you can only do in the particular country you wish to visit.

For example, you can only see the Vatican if you go to Rome, but you can spend time on the beach in any country.

To help you decide what to see consider these points:

● What are your main interests? For example: museums, ancient sites, sporting activities. Put them in order of priority.

● How much time do you have? Remember that some cities, like Paris, could keep you occupied for two weeks but you can see the highlights of others, like Brussels for example, in half a day.

● How much money do you have? Some countries are very expensive, other are cheap.

● Are you travelling with others? It's important that everyone should have a say in what they want to see.

An easy way to plan an itinerary

I would always recommend that you use an itinerary. Not that this should plan things right down to the time and the minute, but you should have a general idea of where you want to be on any particular day. You can always change it, but it will help to get the most from your trip.

Step 1

Start by sitting down and making a list of all the places you would like to see. If there is more than one of you, divided the time away by the number of people, and each plan an itinerary for however many days you each have.

Step 2

When you have your list obtain a large map of the area you wish to travel to. The *Daily Express* Large World Map is very good for this purpose. You can buy it at most bookshops. Stick a map pin or drawing pin at each town or city you wish to visit.

Step 3

Next, take a piece of string! Using a pen make an ink mark at each point which corresponds to 500 miles on your map. If you are using the map above you would make a mark every 25mm or thereabouts. You can cut the length of string according to the time you have for travelling.

Step 4

Now the fun begins! Put the string around all the pins in what seems to be the most direct route. Try several variations until you find the most 'economic' arrangement, *ie* the route that allows you to visit as many places as possible whilst travelling the shortest distance.

Although you will find that this arrangement isn't foolproof, since you can't easily travel between some places that seem close together on a map, it is *much* better than just taking things at random.

Step 5

Once you have obtained your list of destinations, in the *order* you wish to visit them, look at what you are going to do in each place and how long it will take: one day, two days, seven days and so on. From this you can plan a basic itinerary, comprising a list of places to visit and the time you will be spending there.

Step 6

Finally, at this stage you should start to think about *how* you are going to get from place to place on your route. There is some more advice on this later in this book.

TRAVELLING ON A BUDGET

Finding cheap travel

Cheap air travel
Never discount air travel because it seems expensive. It is often actually cheaper mile-for-mile than the local bus! Although you probably won't want to spend all your trip jetting around it can be a good idea if you want to get out to a far-flung area quickly. One good idea is to travel out by air and travel back at your leisure by land.

To get the cheapest air travel always book with care. Never telephone the airline or walk into your local travel agent to make a booking. Go to a discount air ticket outlet. You will see lots of these advertising in the Sunday newspapers. This is all quite safe; as long as you obtain your ticket when you pay for it, and your travel is with an IATA member airline, you will not lose your money if either the agent or the airline (or both) fail.

Always travel **off peak**. There is a huge difference between travelling at peak times, when business people want to travel, and off peak. The cheapest flights are usually during the night.

Next, always ask for a **discount**. This is ideal if you are a student or under 25. Just asking for a discount can be enough to encourage the agent to 'invent' one just to make the sale – but you do have to ask.

If you can, consider an unusual **route**. Journeys which involve stop-overs and round-about trips can often be much cheaper than direct flights as airlines price more keenly on these routes.

Finally, always check to see if a seat is available on a **charter flight**. These are aimed at holidaymakers and so are usually considerably cheaper than scheduled flights which are aimed at business travellers. Also check out the deals offered by the new no-frills airlines such as Easyjet, Go, Virgin Express and Ryanair.

Cheap rail travel
Train travel is certainly one of the nicest ways of travelling, as you get to see the sights and meet the people as you travel. It is cheap, being heavily subsidised in many countries. In some countries, like Switzerland, it is also incredibly reliable and even in the third world, where it isn't, the low cost more than makes up for it.

The best way of getting cheap rail travel is to always book in advance where possible, preferably before leaving home. It is almost always cheaper this way than simply turning up at the station.

At the planning stage, ask if there is a **tourist** or **discount pass**. Many national railway companies have a tourist or discount pass which works out much cheaper than buying individual tickets. Some of these are obscure, so always ask around.

Always use special tickets, such as **Inter Rail** or **Eurail** in Europe. These are normally incredible bargains, *but* only if you plan to do a lot of travelling by rail. They are not recommended if you plan to take just a single journey.

In most countries non-express or stopping trains are almost always much cheaper, and you get to see a lot more of the countryside. Another way to look at this is that express trains sometimes carry a steep supplement.

As with air travel, always choose less popular routes. Popular routes from major city to major city are often more expensive since they are heavily used by business travellers. You can often get a much cheaper ticket by travelling to a nearby town and then taking the bus, or even by travelling out from a suburban station rather than the city centre. You can also discover some nice out-of-the-way spots this way too!

Cheap road travel

Road travel can be a pleasant way of travelling in that it lets you see plenty of the country you are visiting. However, even on express coach services, long journeys can take a long, long time due to poor road, congestion or just drivers who are in no rush to get to their destination. Before considering a coach trip also consider how long it is realistically going to take.

One good piece of advice with road travel is that you should **travel last minute** for the best bargains. Unless you really want to travel a particular route, at a particular time, leave it until you want to travel. You can often get bargains, especially at foreign bus stations, where many operators compete for your business and there is rarely a shortage of seats.

Secondly, always go for a **return ticket**. This usually works out much cheaper than a single ticket if you are likely to use the return. If you do not use the return you may be able to sell it to other travellers once you reach your destination.

Again, always shop around. There is stiff competition in most countries, and you may find a big difference between the nationally-owned coach company and private operators. The newest coaches will also be dearer, although the advantage is that they offer a better degree of safety.

Non-express or **stopping coaches** are usually much cheaper, plus you get to see even more of the countryside. Another way to look at this is that express coaches and 'executive' services often carry a supplement.

Finally, always ask for a discount. Most operators give discounts to students and if they are small, private operators you can get a discount even if you are not a student or don't have the appropriate identification.

Finding free travel

Hitchhiking
Hitchhiking can be an excellent way of travelling as it is free, or almost free, often quite comfortable, and you also get to mix with the local people. On the minus side, of course, it can be quite unreliable and also dangerous in some places.

Before hitchhiking for all or part of your trip, always do your homework. Find out if hitchhiking is:

● possible

● and safe.

Women should note that it is usually easier for them to get lifts, but not always safe, certainly not if alone and possibly not even if travelling in pairs.

Always plan your route. It may be a casual way of travelling but you will do better if you know where you want to go and where you can get lifts. It is always important to stand where drivers can stop. Remember that stopping on motorways and equivalent high speed roads is illegal in almost every country. Plan your trip so that one lift will end where it will be easy to get another, *ie* at a service area rather than a motorway junction.

It always pays to look clean and respectable, and to dress as smartly as your circumstances allow. Lorry drivers might not mind picking up a scruffily dressed backpacker but it will certainly reduce the number of lifts you get in cars!

Always put **safety** first. If you are in any doubts about the motives of the driver always demand that they stop, and get out immediately.

Organised hitchhiking
Hitchhiking need not be a haphazard business. In some countries there

are hitchhiking clubs. These clubs charge a small fee, but will match you up with any drivers who are also members of the club and who are going your way. You can often find out about these clubs from tourist offices or on university campuses.

Cycling
Cycling is worth considering if you are a keen cyclist and reasonably fit. The main advantage is that it is cheap and maintenance is easy in most countries. You will, though, be very restricted in what you can take.

If you are considering this method then check out the situation before leaving. Some countries are very pro-cycling, especially France and the Netherlands. Spain, Italy and Germany are also quite cyclist-friendly. They offer good roads, and even special cycle tracks, and hostels and hotels usually have somewhere to store your bike. In countries such as Greece or Portugal the roads can be poor and special provision for cyclists unknown.

The cheapest method is to take your own bike. However, if you don't want to cycle all the way you could consider **renting** a bike for part of the journey. This is possible in many places, including at most railway stations in France, the Netherlands and some other countries.

If you are planning a longer stay then buying a **secondhand** bike once you arrive and selling it before you come home can work out very inexpensive indeed.

If you cycle, plan your route carefully before you go. Don't attempt more than 30 miles per day unless you are an experienced cyclist. Plan your route around railway lines and stations. If you want a break from cycling it's easy to transport your bike by train, but not so easy by air or coach! Always take a map which is detailed enough to show cycle tracks and side roads. This should be a minimum scale of 1:25,000, otherwise you'll find yourself planning a journey that involves too many main roads.

Finally, be sure to get insurance, as there is a higher risk of being involved in an accident or suffering theft when cycling. If you are travelling outside western Europe check what customs restrictions there are on temporarily importing a cycle.

Tour escort and rep work
Some package holiday companies need **escorts** or **representatives** to escort coach or rail tours, or work in overseas resorts.

If you are presentable and mature and have experience of working with people, even if only in a part time job, you might be able to get a temporary job or a one-off journey.

For this type of work look at the ads in the *Overseas Jobs Express* newspaper.

Car delivery

Another free travel possibility is to offer to drive a car to someone's holiday home, for example in Spain or Italy. You would not normally expect to be paid but you would expect your customer to pay for all insurance, petrol and road tolls. Place an advert in your local paper in advance of the summer season.

In the USA there are official **driveaway** organisations which can organise a trip for you.

Driving jobs

Some haulage and long distance removals companies hire drivers on temporary or one-off contracts to deliver loads, mainly across Europe. If you can't drive then you might be employed as a driver's mate to help with loading and unloading. A quick phone call to all haulage and removals companies in the local *Yellow Pages* may turn up some possibilities.

Whilst you would normally expect to be paid, an offer to do the job free, in return for travel, could prove very tempting to these companies.

Travel writing

If you have a flair for writing, offer an article or report on your chosen destinations to newspapers and magazines which cover travel subjects. Then approach companies that run holidays to your chosen destination, airlines, hoteliers and so on offering to include them in your article or review in exchange for free travel or accommodation. A letter of introduction from a well-known newspaper or magazine can open many doors that would otherwise remain closed.

Yacht crewing

Privately owned, and charter yachts and barges frequently take on deck hands to help with cooking, cleaning and general maintenance. This work is often lowly paid or unpaid, but you do receive free travel and accommodation.

Such jobs can be obtained by reading the yachting and boating press and asking around at marinas.

Little known sources of cheap travel

The following companies specialise in supplying all types of travel tickets at the keenest possible prices. They are also well established, so offering a degree of protection for your money.

Campus Travel. Has thirty-six branches around the UK. The main one is at 52 Grosvenor Gardens, London SW1W 0AG. Tel: (020) 7730 3402.

Council Travel. Has offices around Europe. The UK office is at 28a Poland Street, London W1V 3DB. Tel: (020) 7287 3337.

STA. Has branches around the UK. Head office is Priory House, 6 Wrights Lane, London W8 6TA. Tel: (020) 7938 4711.

Trailfinders. Has branches around the UK. Head office is 42 Earls Court Road, London W8 6EJ. Tel: (020) 7938 3366.

WEXAS International. 45-49 Brompton Road, London SW3 1DE. Tel: (020) 7589 3315.

Finding cheap accommodation

Discount hotel accommodation

Even if you are on a tight budget never think that you won't be able to afford a hotel. Hotels in many countries are cheaper than in others and, by booking your room carefully, you can often save a small fortune on what is known as the **rack rate**, the advertised nightly charge.

First of all, avoid booking in advance if possible. The best rates are usually to be had on the spot, by shopping around. If you want the peace of mind of booking your next night's accommodation in advance, then only book for one night and check local rates once you arrive.

Again, always do your homework. **Tourist guides** often include lists of hotels and many **tourist offices** will supply a free list on request. Once you arrive you can phone or visit suitable hotels, rather than waste time walking the streets.

Once you arrive, always *ask* for a **discount**! This is the norm in many countries but can still work even where it isn't. Avoid paying the rack rate. Telephone first if you find face-to-face bargaining difficult. Make use of **discount cards** and **frequent-user passes** where available. Avoid booking through national booking centres, airport and railway stands and tourist offices.

Note that some hotels and hotel chains, such as Formule 1 in

France, charge per room not per person. Sharing can reduce the cost to a tiny amount each.

Finally, ask if there is a price without breakfast, which is usually much cheaper than just the cost of the food.

Youth hostels
You will find that **youth hostels** exist in most countries around the world. The tourist office of each country can normally supply a list of youth hostels in the area.

The International Youth Hostel Federation (IYHF) has 5,000 hostels worldwide. Hostels can normally be used by non-members but it makes sense to join your relevant national youth hostel association, **YHA**, as the membership is usually very little and non-members are frequently charged more per night. All the hostels you can use are listed in their *Guide to Budget Accommodation* which can be bought at most bookshops.

In the UK the relevant IYHF addresses are:

Scottish Youth Hostels Association, 7 Glebe Crescent, Stirling FK8 2JA. Tel: (01786) 51181.

Youth Hostels Association (England & Wales), 8 St Stephen's Hill, St Albans, Herts AL1 2DY. Tel: (01727) 55215.

IYHF hostels can usually be used by people of all ages, though those under 26 get priority at busy times. At busy times your stay may be restricted, often to three nights.

Private houses
Lodging in private houses can be a good way of staying that you may not have thought about. It is usually quite cheap, with the added advantage that you get to stay a while as part of the local community too.

The main difficulty with lodging in private houses is that it is difficult to find out about them in advance. You should ask the tourist offices of the countries you wish to visit if they have any lists, as some of them do. If not, the only option is to wait until you arrive and then go in search of suitable lodgings. It helps to find out and remember the local term for bed and breakfast for example, in Germany look for Zimmer Frei or Fremdenzimmer.

Camping
Camping is worth considering as a means of providing cheap accom-

modation. However, its main limitations are that you have to depend to some degree on the weather, and your gear also takes up a lot of luggage space.

The availability of **camp sites** varies from country to country as in some places it is more popular than others. So always plan ahead, and obtain details of sites from tour guides and tourist offices.

Although local laws vary, it is either illegal or frowned upon to camp rough in many countries without the landowner's permission. The main exception to this is most of Scandinavia where it is a legal *right*. Farmers will often give you permission but, in most places, camping on the beach will frequently attract the attention of the local police.

Some campsites expect you to have a **Camping Carnet** although, strictly, it is not a legal requirement in any country. This provides insurance for your equipment and also serves as a form of ID. Some campsites will, otherwise, expect to keep your passport during your stay. In the UK you can obtain a Camping Carnet from:

The Camping and Caravanning Club, Green Fields House, Westwood Way, Coventry CV4 8SH. Tel: (024) 7669 4995.

Caravan Parks
Caravan and trailer parks often rent out caravans on a nightly basis. These are very cheap early and late in the season. Ask the tourist office.

Live-in accommodation
If you are willing to do a few days work here and there you could get a job, for example, in a hotel, that provides accommodation.

Universities and college
Many rent out their halls of residence during vacations. Just ask on the local campus.

Temporary summer accommodation
In some countries youth organisations set up temporary summer dormitories to cater for the influx of summer visitors. This accommodation will probably only be basic, such as in a community hall, or gym, but it will be very cheap. Ask the local tourist office.

Pubs and bars
These sometimes rent out rooms. Ask, as they do not always advertise.

Overnight trains

These offer a very cheap place to stay, although they can be uncomfortable and risky from a security point of view. Think twice about paying out for a sleeping birth, as it can work out more costly than a modest hotel room.

Finding free accommodation

It is possible to get free accommodation during your travels. Of course, this may be quite basic and really only for the more adventurous backpacker. However, a few nights in this free accommodation could save you a great deal of money, as well as being an interesting experience!

Ways to enjoy free accommodation

● Farmer's barns and outbuildings. A realistic possibility in summer. Some farmers are willing to give you permission to do this, especially in quieter country areas where not much else is available.

● Charity hostels. These are always a possibility if you are stuck, especially in cities. Some of them offer quite good accommodation too. You might, however, be expected to attend a religious service or undergo some kind of counselling.

● Churches. Churches in some areas allow needy travellers to stay on their premises, or in church halls and so on. Ask for the local clergyman.

● Private homes. It is sometimes possible to stay in private homes free by getting to know people in pubs, bars and so on. This is more likely in rural areas where people are usually more hospitable. Obviously this needs to be done with care, especially if a lone traveller.

● Sleeping rough. Is an option that many travellers consider from time to time. Choose your location with care, making sure that your chosen spot is as safe as possible. Sleeping rough is either illegal or frowned upon in most places, and sleeping in public parks or on beaches often attracts police attention very quickly. Airports, railway stations and bus stations are possibilities and you're unlikely to be turned away if you have a ticket for onward travel.

MORE WAYS TO TRAVEL CHEAPLY

● Plan your route so as to avoid having to change it. Changes can work out expensive.

● Have a daily budget, £20 or whatever, and stick to it. To make this easier know approximately how much your £20 is in the currency of the country you are visiting.

● Make a note of what you spend so that you can stick to your budget. Don't be tempted to borrow from one day so that you can overspend on another.

● Look for 'honeypots'. They may be a bit touristy but you can do lots of different things without spending a lot on travel. For example, in Athens you can enjoy the culture, spend a day on the beach at Glyfada and share Greek village life by taking a short, 30-minute bus trip out of the city.

● Don't plan to travel every day. It eats into your budget more than almost anything else.

● Make use of cheap or free accommodation, such as sleeping on coaches or trains. Also consider camping, although remember it will take up most of your luggage space.

● Have one large meal a day rather than lots of snacks which are overpriced in almost every country.

● Look for free methods of entertainment, such as ancient sites rather than museums, and music bars rather than nightclubs.

● Travel in good weather wherever possible. It *always* works out cheaper in terms of food, clothes and entertainment.

● Travel early or late. There are more cheap travel and accommodation bargains to be had May-June and in September than in July and August.

● Pay for what you can before you go. Then it is not as easy to overspend.

● Consider taking a credit card. If you are visiting several countries you won't have to keep paying out to change one type of foreign currency into another and so on. If you're worried about running up a large debt, put your money into the account before you go.

● When changing money, change everyone's cash together as this will mean that you only pay one transaction charge and you may even get a higher exchange rate for larger sums.

● If you're going as a group share things which you don't need one each of, such as a camera. This way you'll have more space to carry things that you won't have to buy on the way, such as food.

● Avoid staying in popular tourist towns, cities and resorts, which are always overpriced. Instead, base yourself a few miles away and travel in by bus. You'll save a small fortune.

● Buy your travel tickets, excursions and entry tickets where the locals buy them (ask!) rather than at smart travel agencies and tourist offices where tourists shop.

● Buy food, drink and gifts in back street shops, which are usually much cheaper. Try telling the shopkeeper you are living in his/her town for a few months, as shops in some resorts operate a dual pricing system for residents and tourists.

● If you're travelling as a group look for hotels, hostels and campsites which charge per room, or per tent rather than per person as this will work out much cheaper.

● Look for activities and entertainments aimed at students. These are almost always cut-priced. There is nothing to say you have to be a student in that country. In many places you don't even have to be a student to claim a student discount if you just ask for it!

● Avoid anything aimed at tourists as it is usually overpriced.

● Talk to your fellow travellers. People who have been in your chosen destination for a few days or weeks, and who are about to leave, will know about all the best deals and cheapest places to go.

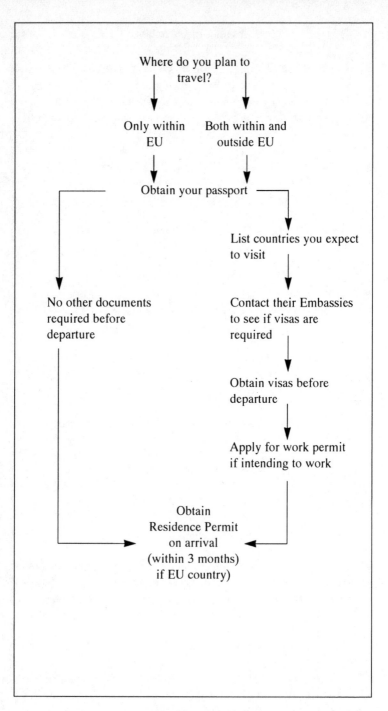

Fig. 4. Obtaining visas and permits.

OBTAINING PASSPORTS, VISAS AND PERMITS

Passports
British citizens should note that a **full passport** is now required to travel to any country outside the UK. The British Visitor's Passport no longer exists.

Applying for a passport
In the UK, passport application forms can be obtained from your nearest main post office. The application can then be returned direct to the passport office. If you wish, applications can be lodged at post offices and certain nominated travel agents, who will check the application before sending it to the passport office.

Apply in plenty of time: at least twelve weeks before you wish to go abroad, longer if you wish to visit a country that requires a **visa**.

Visas
EU citizens travelling to another EU country do not need any sort of visa. The EU countries are: Austria, Belgium, Denmark, Finland, France, Germany, Greece, Ireland, Italy, Luxembourg, Netherlands, Portugal, Spain, Sweden and the UK.

EU citizens travelling outside the EU *may* need a visa, even if travelling as a tourist. If you intend to work a visa will *definitely* be needed.

Non-EU citizens may require a visa to visit any of the countries, EU and non-EU, covered in this book. Since regulations are complex and liable to change you should check with the embassies of the countries you wish to visit.

Applying for a visa
If a visa is needed you can often obtain it at the border, but it is usually easier to obtain it in your own country before leaving home. Apply to the relevant embassy. Most embassies issue visas by post but require at least four weeks' notice. If there is insufficient time you can often apply by going to the embassy (check opening times before travelling as they often open their visa sections only part time), or use a **visa service**, although this can be expensive.

It is a good idea to obtain visas for any countries which require them if you simply *think* you might visit them. It will save time later.

Some visa agencies in London are:

Rapid Visa Service, 131-135 Earls Court Road, London SW5 9RH. Tel: (020) 7373 3026.

Thames Consular Services, 548 Chiswick High Road, London W4 4HS. Tel: (020) 8995 2492.

Thomas Cook Passport and Visa Service, 45 Berkeley Street, London W1A 1EB. Tel: (020) 7408 4141.

Permits

If you are taking a longer trip you should note that, although EU citizens do not require permits to visit or work in other EU countries, they do require **residence permits** if staying for over three months.

These can be obtained at the local town hall, police station or alien's office. You will need to produce evidence that you have sufficient financial means to support yourself (*ie* money in a bank account), although this amount varies from country to country.

CHOOSING WHERE TO TRAVEL

Travelling around Europe

Pros

The chief attractions of Europe are that it is nearby, easy and still relatively inexpensive to travel to. There is a lot to see in a relatively (in world terms) small area and even the most unadventurous traveller shouldn't find it too intimidating.

A significant advantage of travelling with the European Union countries is that you are allowed to work without the need for a visa or work permit, so this can be a good way of boosting your funds.

Cons

On the minus side remember that travel in Europe is seasonal. A lot of places have inclement weather. Similarly, in summer many places can be extremely busy. You will also find that the fashionable hotspots, such as the South of France, Switzerland and so on, are extremely expensive.

Handy reference

For more information on budget travelling in Europe see *Backpacking Round Europe* (How To Books).

Travelling in the USA

Pros

The USA ranks as a highly attractive destination for gap year students.

There is certainly no shortage of things to see and do. Plus, the USA is well geared to the needs of the budget traveller with food, travel and accommodation being very competitively priced.

Cons
One of the disadvantages of travelling in the USA is the great distance and hence the cost, cheap though US travel often is.

However, the main disadvantage of the US as a gap year destination is that foreign nationals are *not* in any circumstances allowed to work unless participating in an organised programme, such as an au pair or on a summer camp, and places on these schemes are limited. If therefore, you wish to work and travel in the USA you must plan well ahead.

Handy reference
For more information on working longer term in the USA see *Getting a Job in America* and *Living & Working in America* (How To Books).

Travelling in Africa

Pros
Africa is still one of the great unexplored areas of the world. Cheaper flights have made it much more accessible lately and it is starting to come within the reach of the budget traveller. If you like the idea of Africa remember that it is a very big place, including countries as diverse as Ethiopia and South Africa.

Cons
On the minus side it is not easy to travel independently in Africa and it can even be dangerous. There is also a lot of red tape when travelling anywhere in this continent.

You are unlikely to be able to work to fund a trip through Africa. Voluntary work opportunities are mostly only for those with some relevant skills and experience to offer.

Travelling in the Far East

Pros
In the last few years the Far East has become cheaper and also easier to travel through than ever before. This is a booming part of the world which offers a combination of old traditions and vast modern cities.

Hundreds of thousands of budget travellers flock to locations such as Hong Kong, Thailand and India each year, and even China is now more accessible. With the exception of Japan, the Far East is also a fairly inexpensive destination.

The Far East also offers a few employment opportunities, such as in teaching English, which might help to finance your travels, although it is no longer as easy to get this work as it once was.

Cons
There are a few disadvantages to Far Eastern travel. There are health risks in some places and some areas are considered unsafe, so check carefully when planning your trip.

Travelling in Australia

Pros
Australia is a very popular destination for those travelling during a gap year. There is a lot to see and do and the social life is a major attraction.

However, by far the major attraction of Australia is that it is relatively easy for young travellers aged 18-25 to obtain a **working holiday visa**. This lasts for approximately one year, and allows you to take casual and temporary work to subsidise your visit. Details of the scheme are available from the Australian High Commission (address at the end of the book) and it costs approximately £75.

Cons
The main drawbacks to Australia are the distance and cost of travel both to and within the country. Casual work isn't as easy to find as it once was.

Handy reference
For more information on employment and staying in Australia see *Living & Working in Australia* and *Getting a Job in Australia* (How To Books).

PLANNING A ROUND-THE-WORLD TRIP

One of the travel opportunities you might consider is a **round-the-world** or **RTW** trip. This is one opportunity that you might never have again, due to lack of time if not lack of money. However, this is a major undertaking. You will need to plan carefully to get the best from your trip and to manage it on a budget.

There are very few dos and don'ts for a round-the-world trip. Apart from travelling it also offers the opportunity to:

● work

● do voluntary work

● take part in an exchange

● or even study.

Answering your questions

How much times does it take to go round the world?

This is up to you. Most people fly most of the way so you won't even need a full year, but three months is probably a reasonable minimum and even then you won't be able to see everything.

What is it likely to cost?

The cheapest round-the-world air ticket is, and has been for the last couple of years, about £1,100. This would allow you to visit about six destinations. The cheapest accommodation and food costs are likely to be at least as much again, assuming a three-month journey.

The longer the duration and the greater the number of stops the more the ticket will cost.

How should I plan my journey?

This is to some extent dictated by the conditions attached to RTW air tickets. Usually you have to travel round the world in one direction. Most RTW deals seem to be for easterly journeys, for some reason. You can't backtrack, can't visit any destination more than once, and must continue your journey from the same city in which you arrived on each stage.

There are an infinite number of combinations, of course, but a typical RTW trip starting from London would be: Athens – Egypt – India – Hong Kong – Australia – San Francisco – New York – London.

How far should I plan my trip?

You will need to more or less fix and keep to an itinerary, in order to comply with the conditions of the ticket. Also, remember that many countries require visas which are best obtained before leaving.

What about travel companions?

An RTW trip is best enjoyed with a companion, and much safer too. If you don't know of anyone try advertising for a companion in the link-up section of *Overseas Jobs Express*.

What about health?

Check with your doctor's surgery at least three months before travelling. Tell them which countries you are visiting and they will be able to tell you if any vaccinations or other health precautions are either compulsory or advised.

Alternatively contact a British Airways clinic. Tel: (020) 7436 2625.

What about insurance?

You *must* take full medical insurance, as few countries provide visitors with free medical treatment. Even in Europe only a limited amount of treatment is provided free to nationals of other European countries.

Where can I get RTW air tickets?

Any travel agent can supply round-the-world tickets but Campus Travel, Council Travel and STA Travel (addresses given on page 40) all specialise in providing this sort of travel.

Handy reference

For more information on travelling around the world see *How to Travel Round the World* (How To Books).

CASE HISTORY

David gets on his bike

David decided to cycle around France and Spain during part of his gap year.

'My decision to travel was made due to my passion for cycling as much as anything else. I knew it was a case of now or never. Plus, having worked hard to get good A levels I did feel that I needed a break and a chance to 'catch up with myself' before going on to the next stage of my life.

'I had an excellent time cycling in France and Spain. One of the advantages of this type of travelling is that it cost me very little. Probably, though, it would only appeal to keen cyclists. If you do intend to travel it is important to choose a type of travel and a destination which really will appeal to you.

'Other benefits of my travels are that I can now make myself understood quite well in both French and Spanish, which might come in useful in the future. I also feel a lot more capable and a lot less stressed when dealing with difficult situations. Compared with finding a place to stay for a man and his bike in Barcelona at 10 at night, finding research for that difficult essay is easy!'

CHECKLIST

1. Is travelling really for you?

2. What do you want to see?

3. What do you want to do?

4. How will you travel?

5. How can you buy cheaper travel?

4
Working Opportunities

SPENDING SOME TIME WORKING

What are the chances of finding work?

Working for a while can be a tempting way to spend your gap year. Not only will your job finance other activities on your gap year itself, but you may even be able to save money to help get your college year off to a flying start as well!

However, do be realistic about your chances of finding work. Without any relevant experience or qualifications you may be mainly restricted to casual work, which is often hard to find and not well paid.

What could you do?

Again this is an area in which you need to be realistic. Even if your A levels are excellent they are not necessarily a passport into an interesting, well-paid job at this point. Indeed, they may be of little or no use at all in this respect.

You should make the choice between the following types of work.

A job that has no career potential

Casual work, lowly paid but with no responsibilities. This may be OK for making money and marking time but it will not impress admissions tutors nor future employers.

A job that has career potential

For example, if you hope to start a career in banking you might apply for a job in a bank. This could also be a good 'play safe' option. If you have doubts about whether to go on to college you could always stay in this job after your gap year.

A job that will contribute towards your course

This is the best type of job to go for. If the job adds to your personal or practical skills, or provides you with another aspect on the subject you are going to study, then this will certainly help your future prospects.

CHOOSING THE RIGHT TYPE OF WORK

It's one thing to just walk into the first job that you are offered. However, before you do this stop and think. These are some of the points to consider:

● Is the job temporary or permanent, full or part time? Will there be room for other gap year activities too?

● What practical skills will it give me? For example, the opportunity to work with computers.

● What personal skills will it give me? For example, the confidence to deal with people at all levels or to supervise staff.

● Will it give me any useful qualifications?

● Will it give me any relevant experience?

● Will I be able to come back to it in the university vacations? If you can then this will help supplement your income and give you a useful head start over the other students looking for holiday jobs.

● Is it at home or away? A job that takes you away from home for a time is generally regarded as more character building but it almost always costs more to live away from home.

FINDING WORK

How to find a job

Here are some useful tips if you are new to the experience of job seeking.

Newspapers

Newspapers are an obvious source of jobs. Be sure to look in all your local and regional newspapers and also the national press. No matter what you might have heard always reply as soon as possible. These vacancies are usually heavily over-subscribed.

Trade journals

If you are looking for a job in a particular trade or profession, perhaps one linked to your course, then don't forget the relevant trade journals. They often have vacancies for trainees.

The job centre
Mostly handles vacancies for unskilled and semi-skilled work. Worth a look but there are probably many more jobs in your area that aren't listed here than are.

Private employment agencies
These are a growing breed. Some do handle unskilled or semi-skilled casual work. However, if you have some relevant skills or experience, *eg*, secretarial, you will get a better job at a specialist agency.

Asking around
There is a lot to be said for the direct approach of job-hunting when looking for work. This is because many employers do not have a vacancy as such but are often tempted once help is offered at busy times. So simply decide what type of work you wish to do and ask around. Ask your friends and family if there are any jobs available at their places of work as a surprising number of jobs are found on this basis.

Letters and phone calls
Writing letters and making phone calls to companies in your area can be a very successful way of finding a job. When you make an approach don't ask the employer if they have any jobs suitable for a 'student' or a 'gap year'. Instead, focus on what you think *you* can offer *them*.

Applying for a job
Here are some useful tips if you are new to the experience of applying for a job.

Written applications
If writing, follow the instructions given in the advertisement exactly. The visual quality of your application – good writing paper, tidy hand-writing, correct spelling and no mistakes – count for a great deal. Some employers cut down their workload by simply discarding applications which look messy.

Application forms
Again, pay attention to neatness and accuracy. The best way of handling application forms is to make a photocopy, complete the copy first, perfect it and then fill in the original.

CVs
It is always a good idea to have a CV, or *curriculum vitae*, handy to send if requested. The sample on page 58 shows how to set this out. A CV should always be typewritten, or prepared on a wordprocessor, and take up one side of one sheet of A4 paper only.

Telephone applications
Telephoning allows you to cover a lot of ground in a short period of time. It also allows you to get in ahead of those who write letters.

One of the most important aspects of telephoning is to make sure you speak to the right person. In a small company ask to speak to the owner or manager, since they are likely to be the only person entitled to hire staff. In a larger company ask for the personnel department. Whatever you do don't ask the telephonist or just anyone who happens to answer the phone, since hiring is almost certainly nothing to do with them and, more often than not, they will be too busy with their own work to help you out.

Finding a part time job

If you do not want to be tied to a full time job you might consider getting a part time one instead. Indeed, these seem to be more plentiful and easier to come by than full time positions nowadays. You might even decide to take two or more part time jobs, and tailor your working hours to your own needs and leave time over for other activities.

Here are some useful tips on part time employment.

● More part time jobs are probably found through personal contacts, asking around and making speculative telephone calls, than other methods.

● A part time job is probably less likely to impress future employers and admission tutors.

● You may be asked to work longer/shorter hours, split shifts and so on. This makes it harder to fit in other activities.

● Part time jobs are very often temporary too. This means your job can come to an end at little or no notice, and you probably won't be entitled to the same benefits as permanent staff such as staff discounts, holiday pay, sick pay and so on.

CURRICULUM VITAE

Name:	Jane Thomas
Address:	9 The Drive, Anytown, Dyfed AB1 2CD
Telephone:	0123 456789
Date of Birth:	2 February 19XX
Nationality:	British

Education:
199X-199X
Anytown Comprehensive School.
GCSEs:
English Language (C), Geography (C),
History (C), Communication Studies (C),
Mathematics (C), French (C), Science (C).

199X-199X,
Anytown College.
A Levels:
English Language, Geography, History.
(Awaiting results of examination.)

Work Experience:
2U Fashions Ltd, Anytown.
Saturday Sales Assistant, Fashion Store,
June 199X-March 199X.

Childcare Experience:
I babysit for family friends two evenings each week. I also help at the Peter Pan Playscheme which is run by our local church during the school holidays.

Interests & Activities:
My interests include foreign travel, riding and socialising with family and friends at weekends.

Other Information:
I hold a clean current driving licence.

Fig. 5. A sample curriculum vitae.

Some types of work to try

Office work
Not as easy to get as other types. However, the experience of working in an office, using modern office equipment and so on can help polish up your study skills. A short course in computer skills, preferably Windows, will significantly increase your job prospects here.

Factory/industrial work
This type of work is likely to be more useful if it has a link with your future career in some way.

Retail work
Jobs in shops are widely available but less likely to help your future prospects. Aiming for a supervisory or management post will help develop your organisational and man/woman management skills.

Domestic and childcare work
If you are interested in au pairing abroad this is covered later in the book.

Hotels and catering
Good for summer employment, but less likely to help your future prospects.

Seasonal and summer jobs
Again, these are less likely to help your future prospects.

Voluntary work
Opportunities for voluntary work are covered in Chapter 6.

Gap year placements
A small number of large companies now have work placements which are intended specifically for gap year students. These include Marks and Spencer, National Power and Royal Insurance, amongst others.

With the Marks and Spencer scheme, for example, you can spend up to six months working for the company at the start of the gap year. You can then leave to pursue other interests or, if suitable, join the company on a permanent basis, or take an option to join the company after you have taken your degree course as a graduate trainee. Throughout the programme you will be fully trained, gain hands-on work experience and be paid too.

The Manager,   Charlotte James,
Sitters Au Pair Agency,   1 The Road,
1 The Place,   Anytown,
London SW1A 0AA   Berkshire RG1 1AA
                                              Tel: 0123 999999
                                            1 December 199X

Dear Sir,

Please find enclosed my completed application form and other
documents applying for an au pair placement in France
commencing in May 199X.

I look forward to hearing from you shortly, and if you have
any queries regarding my application please do not hesitate
to contact me.

Yours faithfully,

Charlotte James

Fig. 6. A sample application letter.

Although the number of companies offering such placements is growing it is still small and places are always in short supply. If you are interested you should, therefore, contact employers as soon as you have decided to take a gap year. Some, but not all, placements of this type are arranged by:

The Year in Industry (YII), University of Manchester, Simon Building, Oxford Road, Manchester M13 9PL. Tel: (0161) 275 4396.

If you cannot find a place on an organised gap year scheme then it is always worth writing to companies and asking if they would be willing to create a gap year scheme just for you, as this is by no means unknown.

Handy reference
A number of other How To Books cover finding a job in some of the areas above. These include:

Applying for a Job
Finding a Job in Computers
Working in Hotels and Catering
Getting a Job in Travel and Tourism
Getting That Job
How to Work in an Office
How to Work in Retail.

PAY, BENEFITS AND CONTRACTS

Although there is now a minimum rate of pay in the UK always make sure that you have clearly agreed the rate of pay before starting a job, together with any other benefits offered such as meals and accommodation. If they are not free ask what deductions will be made.

Also ask if any deduction will be made for tax or social security. This depends on your weekly wage.

Your contract of employment
You have a right to be issued with a **contract of employment** by your employer when starting your job which will, amongst other things, cover some of the points above. It should also state what notice you have to give or be given. Normally this will vary between seven days and one month.

SUNSHINE HOLIDAYS Plc
Application for Employment

● Please complete every section of this form using a black ballpoint pen. If there is insufficient space to give a complete answer then please attach a separate sheet.

Position applied for: _____

Surname: _____

Forenames: _____

Marital status: Single/Engaged/Married/
        Divorced/Separated/Widowed _____

Date of Birth: _____

Age: _____

Place of Birth: _____

Nationality: _____

Address: _____

_____

Telephone (include area code): _____

Address of parents or guardian (if different): _____

_____

Please give any dates in the near future when you will not be available for interview:

Where did you hear of this vacancy?:

continued

Fig. 7. A sample application form.

UNIFORM DETAILS

Female:	Male:
UK size:	Chest:
Bust:	Waist:
Waist:	Inside leg:
Hips:	Collar:
Height:	Height:

EMPLOYMENT HISTORY

Are you employed at present?   YES/NO

If yes, please state your current employer's name, address, telephone and type of business:

_____

_____

Reason for wishing to leave: _____

Have you previously working in a position which involved dealing with the public and providing them with a service?   YES/NO

If yes, please state your employer, name, address, telephone, type of business and your reason for leaving:

Job 1:   _____

_____

_____

Job 2:   _____

_____

_____

Fig. 7. (continued).

REFERENCES

Please give two employment references:

1. _____

2. _____

May we contact the above individuals/companies after interview?   YES/NO

Have you worked for our company before?   YES/NO

If yes, please state position and reason for leaving:

LANGUAGE ABILITY

Do you speak any foreign languages?   YES/NO

If yes, please state: _____

Where learnt	Level of proficiency	Qualifications

QUALIFICATIONS

Do you have any qualifications which are directly related to the job you are applying for?   YES/NO

If yes, please state:

Subject	Qualification	Grade	Issuing body

Please list any other qualifications below (eg. GCSEs, A-Levels, degrees).

Subject	Qualification	Grade	Issuing body

Fig. 7. (continued).

MEDICAL

Please give details of any illnesses you have suffered within the last 5 years and any current medical conditions:

Please state below your main reasons for applying for this job and what you think you could offer to our company:

I declare that the information on this application is correct. If employment if offered to me, it will be conditional on the receipt of satisfactory references.

Signature: _____ Date:_____

● When completed please return this form to the PERSONNEL DEPARTMENT and attach 2 passport sized photographs to the top right hand corner.

FOR PERSONNEL DEPARTMENT USE ONLY:

Fig. 7. (continued).

CASE HISTORY

Dan gets down to work

Dan decided to spend his gap year working.

'I'd heard lots of horror stories about students who have built up huge debts in their first year and decided, at all costs, that wasn't going to happen to me. My plan was to build up the biggest possible cash reserve before starting on my course.

'From the day I finished my A levels I took every part time and casual job I could get – days, evenings, weekends, whatever. Most of the jobs I took were unskilled, part time jobs which I found very easy to find in my area. Some of them were quite well paid (£5 plus per hour) but none of them were very interesting.

'During the year I managed to save almost £10,000 which, together with my grant and help from my parents, meant that I managed to avoid running up any debts to speak of during my three-year course. In answer to the question 'was it worth it?' I'd say that it definitely was, although I did find it hard to get back to studying after my gap year, plus I don't think that it does my CV any favours either!'

CHECKLIST

1. Do you want to work or do you need to work?

2. Realistically, will you be able to find the work you want?

3. What type of work are you best suited to?

4. How can you improve job-hunting techniques?

5. Have you tried the unusual as well as the usual, as a way of finding work?

5
Finding Work Abroad

ASSESSING THE CHANCES OF FINDING WORK

Spending some time working abroad is a possibility that has become more popular in recent years, especially now that citizens of any of the fifteen EU countries are entitled to take work in any of those countries without a visa or work permit. This is an exciting possibility, giving you a choice of several hundreds of thousands of jobs on an EU-wide basis!

Having realised the possibilities, try to be practical. Remember that unemployment is a problem in almost every other EU country, with very few exceptions. Your chances of finding work will also depend on your ability, or otherwise, to speak the language of the country concerned.

Many travellers look for casual work abroad in summer to supplement their holiday funds.

What could you do?

There are two main options when working abroad for your gap year:

- First, you might decide to aim for a full time job, perhaps of a type that will help you in your course in some way. This will be more difficult to set up and will require good language abilities.

- Second, you might decide to look for casual work. This is a popular option when combined with travelling. It can be quite easy to find in many countries, though is rarely highly paid. Depending on the type of work involved you won't necessarily need to be fluent in the language concerned.

HOW TO FIND A JOB ABROAD

The best ways of finding a job abroad are outlined below.

UK newspapers

Some UK national newspapers advertise jobs abroad, although these are fairly limited in number. *The Daily Telegraph* and *Guardian* have some professional and technical vacancies if you are interested in a traineeship.

However, a better choice of vacancies, including casual and temporary work, is available in specialist newspapers such as *Overseas Jobs Express*.

Foreign Newspapers

Just as in this country, foreign newspapers have a wide selection of job vacancies. It is possible to buy newspapers from other countries in newsagents in the larger towns and cities, or they can also be obtained at some libraries.

Some countries have English language newspapers which carry advertisements for jobs suitable for English speakers. In Greece there is the *Athens News* and in Belgium *The Bulletin*. Foreign embassies and tourist offices can often tell you about these publications.

Direct applications

There is much to be said for making a direct application to employers as a way of finding work abroad. This can be done by:

● telephone

● letter

● or in person.

The latter is particularly suitable if you are taking a working holiday.

Application can be made to both employers in the UK who have jobs abroad, such as travel companies, and employers overseas.

Employment agencies

Employment agencies, whether private or state-run, exists in almost all countries worldwide. As a foreign visitor there is not usually any reason why you cannot use them to find a job, although you would probably be expected to speak the language of the country concerned to some extent.

Citizens of EU countries are fully entitled to use the state employment services in all other European countries. So, for example, you could call into the ANPE in France or the Arbeitsamt in Germany and ask about vacancies. Normally they will expect you to have some langauge ability in the language concerned. They also usually only deal with personal callers.

UK Job Centres

Your local UK Job Centre also keeps details of some vacancies in Europe through the pan-European **EURES** (European Employment Services) network. It may be worth asking if interested, although many of these vacancies are for those with relevant skills/experience and language ability.

Advertising

One less conventional method which can be tried is to place a Situations Wanted advertisement in a foreign newspaper, describing yourself and the job you require. This can be expensive and the chances of success quite slim, but it can be worth trying if you are intent on securing a particular job in a particular place.

An advertisement agency can place your advertisement in foreign newspapers for you.

Frank L. Crane Ltd, 5 Cromer Street, London WC1H 8LS. Tel: (020) 7837 3330. Fax: (020) 7837 0917.

Specialised gap year project agencies

There are a number of specialised agencies which can arrange work placements abroad, either for a few weeks, or a year or more. These placements are often combined with travelling, exchanges, voluntary work or expeditions.

Agencies offering this type of opportunity include Fill The Gap and GAP Activity Projects. (Addresses are given at the end of the book.)

One of the disadvantages of using a specialised agency is that the fees charged by the agency may not be covered by the actual wages earned if, indeed, the work is paid at all.

APPLYING FOR A JOB ABROAD

The procedure for applying for a job abroad is very much the same as applying for a job at home. However, the following tips may be helpful:

● Remember that personal and telephoned applications always get there quicker than written applications.

CURRICULUM VITAE

Name/Nom/Name/Apellidos/Nome:

Address/Adresse/Anschrift/Dirección/Indirizzo:

Tel:

Date of birth/Date de naissance/Geburtsdatum/Fecha de nacimiento/Data di nascita:

Nationality/Nationalité/Staatsangehörigkeit/Nacionalidad/ Cittadinanza:

Education/Etudes/Ausbildungagang/Estudios/Studi:

Work experience/Expérience professionelle/ Berufserfahrung/Experiencia profesional/Esperienza professionale:

Fig. 8. Sample CV with captions in five languages.

Reference/Référence/Referenz/Referencia/Referenza (Attestato)

1.   2.

Interests outside work/Activités extra-professionelles/
Ausserberufliche/Actividades extra-profesionales/
Attività o attitudini extraprofessionali:

Other information/Information supplémentaire/Zusätzlich
information/Información adicional/Informazioni supplementare:

Date/Date/Datum/Fecha/Date:

Fig. 8. (continued).

- Don't assume that the potential employer speaks English. If he/she does they are likely to speak it better than they read it.

- Make every attempt to speak as much of the local language as possible.

- Remember that employers can be wary of 'here today, gone tomorrow' working travellers. Always give the impression that you intend to stay a while.

TYPES OF WORK YOU COULD TRY

Most travellers usually look for casual work, which requires few skills or commitment. Here are some of the jobs you could consider.

Hotels and catering

Hotels are enthusiastic hirers of casual workers. You may be employed as a chambermaid, gardener, porter and so on. If you can speak the local language you may be able to get a job in reception.

Restaurants often need a lot of staff. You may get work as a kitchen porter or washer-up. Again, if you speak the local language you may get a job as a waiter or waitress or as a meeter-and-greeter.

Bars are always in need of part time workers. This is an ideal type of work in tourist resorts. Do note, however, that the popular resorts have more than enough workers in the high season.

Fast food outlets such as McDonalds exist in almost every European country, and often need part time and temporary staff.

Working in tourism

Holiday centres or camps often have vacancies for chambermaids, waiters and waitresses, porters and so on. If you can sing or dance, or teach a sport, you may even be able to get a job as an entertainer or coach.

If you are a determined type of person you may be able to earn money by persuading tourists to eat in certain restaurants, drink in certain bars or even view timeshare properties. Ask the owners if they need a tout. In many resorts casual workers are employed to sell drinks, ice creams, sun beds and parasols on the beach. Note that you usually need a licence to do this.

Office work

Offices frequently have opportunities for temporary workers. However, you would normally need to speak and write the language concerned.

Factory work

There are opportunities here in most countries, although the work may be of a tedious or monotonous nature. This work can most readily be obtained through a local employment agency.

Domestic work

You might be able to work as an au pair or nanny. This mainly applies to women. You stand a better chance of getting this work if you are prepared to stay for a few weeks.

Working in agriculture and farming

Farmers often need a few extra pairs of hands, especially at busy times such as harvest or planting. Pay is usually low but you might get benefits such as food and accommodation free.

Teaching work

One option often considered by those taking a gap year is to spend it teaching English abroad. English language institutes in many countries will take on English language speakers to teach English. This is quite common in Spain, Portugal, Greece, eastern Europe and most of the Far East, especially Japan.

Whether or not you need a teaching qualification to do this work depends on the quality of the school in question. You will increase your chances of getting a job if you first obtain a **TEFL** (Teaching English as a Foreign Language) qualification, such as that offered by the Royal Society of Arts.

Handy reference
You will find more detailed information and addresses on opportunities for taking casual work as you travel in *Backpacking Around Europe* (How To Books).

DEALING WITH RED TAPE

Obtaining a visa

Very few countries allow those from other countries to enter and work, or even to look for a job, without a suitable visa.

The main exceptions to this rule are nationals of EU countries wishing to work in other EU countries, who do not need any sort of visa to work, or look for work, in another EU country. You may, however,

5 January 199X

Personnel Department,
Cambronne Auto,
100 Avenue Branly,
75019 Paris.

Dear Sirs,

Your Advertisement in 'The Times', 5 January 199X.

In reply to your advertisement in today's 'The Times' I wish
to apply for the post of _____

_____

Please find enclosed my C.V.

I hope the enclosed will be of interest and I look forward
to hearing from you.

Yours faithfully,

John Smith.

Encl. C.V.

Fig. 9. An example of a simple application letter
written in both English and French.

John Smith,
1 High Street,
Leeds,
West Yorkshire.
LS1 1AA
Angleterre.

Leeds, le 5 janvier 199X

Référence: Votre annonce dans
'les Echos' no 16.180

Service du personnel,
Cambronne Auto,
100 avenue Branly,
75029 Paris.

Messieurs,

En reponse à votre annonce parue ce jour dans 'les
Echos', je me permets de poser ma candidature au
poste de ....

Veuillez trouvez ci-joint mon curriculum vitae.

Dans l'espoir que vous voudrez bien considérer
favorablement ma demande et dans l'attente de votre
reponse, je vous prie d'agréer. Messieurs,
l'assurance de mes sentiments distingués.

John Smith.

P.J.C.V.

Fig. 9. (continued).

require a residence permit if you intend to live in the country in question for more than three months.

If wishing to work in a country where a visa is required you should make enquiries with the relevant embassy or consulate well in advance. You may find that there are special conditions in many countries and, in others, a visa is very unlikely to be granted. Some countries, such as Australia and the USA, allow a limited number of foreign nationals to take certain types of work according to strict conditions but, in any case, you must obtain your visa before leaving for the country concerned.

Obtaining work permits

The situation on work permits is very similar to that for visas. That is, you will normally require a work permit before taking up a job in any other foreign country. The main exception is citizens of one EU country who wish to work in another, who do not require a work permit.

If wishing to work in a country where a work permit is required you should make enquiries with the relevant embassy or consulate well in advance. You may find that there are special conditions in many countries and, in others, a permit is very unlikely to be granted. Although in some countries you can apply for a work permit once you arrive you must normally apply for it before you enter the country in question.

CASE HISTORY

Harriet and Claire find the best jobs have gone

Harriet and Claire decided to look for a summer job in Tenerife.

'We'd read in several books that there were jobs to be had in bars and restaurants in summer holiday resorts. So, as soon as we finished our last A level, we took a last-minute package holiday to Tenerife with the idea of looking for waitressing jobs.

'By the time we arrived it was too late to look for this type of work. There are not as many vacancies as we thought anyway, and in any case they'd all been taken. All we were offered were jobs trying to persuade holidaymakers to view timeshare resorts. This was incredibly hard work, paid on commission only, but we managed to earn enough each week to pay for our living costs.

'Our advice to anyone thinking of working abroad would be to plan carefully. You can certainly get work in the resorts, but it's not easy. You need to be determined and you probably won't be paid as much as you would at home.'

CHECKLIST

1. Are you being realistic about work abroad?

2. Is the type of work you want available where you want to go?

3. Have you used all the different methods?

4. Always have a contingency plan: what will you do if you can't find a job?

6
Voluntary Work Opportunities

BEING A VOLUNTEER

Is voluntary work for you?

Undertaking voluntary work can be a very appealing way of spending some or all of your year. But take care! Just because you are working for a good cause does not mean it is necessarily right for you, or for the people you will be helping. Many a willing volunteer has caused chaos by volunteering to do the wrong thing.

Voluntary work has both advantages and disadvantages and these are the points to bear in mind when considering it:

The pros

- It can be very rewarding helping others.

- You will learn new and useful skills.

- Experience in voluntary work may impress future employers; it will look good on your CV.

- There is often a chance to work abroad, perhaps in countries you would not otherwise have a chance to visit.

- You will get a chance to do things you could never do in a regular job.

The cons

- Most of the work is either unpaid or low paid.

- Some types of work are quite competitive to get into. You might not always get your first choice.

- Some voluntary work involves more mundane office work, administration and fund raising than 'hands-on' work helping others.

- You may have to give a minimum commitment, such as a full year.

- You may get personally or emotionally involved. It is not nine-to-five work.

- Some voluntary work programmes require you to make a financial contribution.

Only you can decide how much the individual pros and cons matter to you. For example, some people feel that working for a voluntary agency will always be second best to a 'proper' job . For others it is much more rewarding, regardless of what they are paid, and the experience may even help them to get a much better job in future. Take some time to decide for yourself.

WHAT COULD YOU DO?

One of the advantages of voluntary work is that there is something for everyone. But you must take care to match up what is available with what you want. One project might be enjoyable for one person, but a nightmare for another.

As one volunteer said, 'It is best if you have a passion for the work you are doing. And don't do it if you don't at least have a keen interest!'

The range of types of voluntary work is very wide. Helping out with a jumble sale or flag day are just two ways, but there are many others too. Teaching, nursing, building, labouring, office work, fund raising and even just befriending are all types of voluntary work.

There are no divisions to voluntary work as such. But most agencies which have opportunities for voluntary work tend to specialise in a particular type. Some of them are working:

- with the elderly
- with children and young people
- in hospitals
- to relieve poverty
- with the disabled

- in education and training
- in conservation and the environment
- with animals
- in archaeology and history
- with reform and pressure groups
- with religious charities
- in medicine and health
- in disaster relief
- to give advice
- for peace and development
- for minorities
- with the homeless
- on community projects
- with prisoners
- with public service charities.

Some of the most popular opportunities are covered in greater detail later in this section.

WORKING IN THE UK

The UK has one of the largest and most active voluntary sectors. There are voluntary agencies working in almost every sector and ranging from the large, nationally known names such as Oxfam, right down to one-man or one-woman charities. Although most voluntary work is unpaid there are also opportunities for paid work.

The headquarters of most large voluntary agencies are in London. If wishing to work for one of these agencies, find out if they have a local agent, or local projects, so that you can go along for a chat before finally making your application.

WORKING ABROAD

Volunteers can work in almost any country of the world. A lot of work is done in the poorer, third world countries by agencies that are based in the richer countries. In general terms there are fewer opportunities to work internationally than in the UK and many of these jobs are for those with experience of voluntary work in the UK.

Voluntary Service Overseas has many opportunities for overseas voluntary work. However, most opportunities are for those with relevant work experience to offer.

Agencies with overseas opportunities for those without experience include:

● Service Civil International (branches in most countries)

● ATD Fourth World

● International Voluntary Service

● Christian Movement for Peace

● United Nations Association (Wales).

The best advice is to choose your type of work first and the country you wish to work in second.

FINDING VOLUNTARY WORK

The process of finding voluntary work is not exactly the same as when finding other types of work. The main sources are as follows.

Newspapers
It is worth looking in all your local, regional and some of the main national newspapers. However, a number of these vacancies are full time paid positions for those with experience.

The main national newspapers carrying paid vacancies are *The Daily Telegraph* (Mondays), *The Independent* (Thursdays), *The Guardian* (Wednesday and Fridays).

Specialist publications
There are a few specialist publications carrying news and vacancies. These include *Community Care, The Conserver* and *Campaign*. Try *Overseas Jobs Express* if you would like to do voluntary work abroad. *NCVO News* is good for background news.

Voluntary service bureaux
There are now voluntary service bureaux in many towns and cities. These bureaux do not undertake voluntary work themselves as such, but act as a contact point between willing volunteers and voluntary agencies requiring helpers. To contact your local voluntary service bureau look in your telephone directory or *Yellow Pages*.

● The National Association of Volunteer Bureaux can also put you in touch with your local voluntary service bureau. Their address is given at the end of the book.

● The Volunteer Centre UK operates a service called Signposts which can put you in touch with local voluntary agencies and voluntary work projects direct. Their address is also given at the end of the book.

Direct application

If you would like to work for a particular voluntary agency there is nothing to stop you contacting them, either by letter or telephone, and asking if they may be able to make use of your services in some way.

Names, addresses and telephone numbers of voluntary agencies in the UK can be obtained from:

● *The Henderson Top 1,000 Charities*, available at many libraries.

● *The Voluntary Agencies Directory*, available at many libraries and bookshops.

● *Doing Voluntary Work Abroad* (How To Books).

Other sources

Ask your school, careers office or library if they can provide access to the computer database called Youth for Britain. This lists several hundred organisations with a requirement for young volunteers, both at home and abroad.

ADVANTAGES OF WORKING FOR FREE

● It will enhance your CV.

● It may impress admissions tutors and employers.

● It will help develop your personal skills.

● You may learn new practical skills.

● You may have the chance to travel at little or no cost.

● It will broaden your horizons.

● Great personal satisfaction from helping others.

● Many projects offer free accommodation and food.

● You may be able to study for a new qualification whilst working.

● Useful experience of the world of work. You may even discover new career possibilities.

CONSIDERING TYPES OF WORK

This section covers a few of the more popular types of voluntary work you might consider.

Conservation projects

Conservation issues are now becoming increasingly relevant and so the number of opportunities to do this type of work is rising. Organisations involved in this work divide broadly into two types:

● Some are involved with promoting and campaigning on conservation issues.

● Others actually undertake hands-on conservation projects, such as protecting wildlife habitats, or restoring canals or footpaths.

A number of agencies do both types of work.

More information about this type of work can be found in *The Conserver* newspaper and *BBC Wildlife* and *Green* magazines. Some of the agencies involved in conservation include BTCV, the Council for the Protection of Rural England, the Countryside Commission, Friends of the Earth, Greenpeace, the Royal Society for the Protection of Birds (RSPB) and the World Wide Fund for Nature (WWF). The BCTV offers three to twelve month periods working as a volunteer officer, for those with a keen interest in conservation.

Archaeological and cultural projects

Although most governments now take cultural issues more seriously than perhaps they did in the past – the UK now has a government official delegated to oversee the national heritage – it is still the case that a lot of work in this area is done by the voluntary sector. Some of them are involved in hands-on preservation work on archaeological digs or historic buildings. This work involves many activities from excavating, preserving and cataloguing to researching, recreating and organising cultural sites and events.

To find out about this type of work contact the various agencies direct. These include English Heritage and the National Trust. The National Trust owns 300 historic buildings and sites. Most areas have an historical society. *Whitakers Almanack* contains a list of historic monuments, properties and sites.

Work camps

A work camp is usually an event organised by a voluntary organisation for a short period. These are typically held in summer, both within the UK and the rest of the world, especially Europe. They are usually convened to deal with a particular issue in, for example, conservation or the community. The aim is to complete an entire project of real value – such as rebuilding a footpath or creating a community centre – during the period in which the camp operates.

Work camps can be hard work but a lot of fun. They usually provide food and very basic accommodation free, but also a chance to travel and explore the area in which you are located. A charge may be made for the work camp, especially if it is abroad.

To find out about work camp opportunities contact voluntary agencies direct. Major agencies operating work camps include the British Trust for Conservation Volunteers (BTCV) and the United Nations Association (Wales).

Working with children

Voluntary work with children and young people is some of the most demanding but rewarding voluntary work. It is also very wide ranging and once in one sector most voluntary workers tend to specialise, although it is possible to change. Some of the main areas of work are:

● special needs teaching

● social work

● health services

● group leading

- sports/activities instruction

- residential home care.

The work can be ideal for those planning a career in the caring services.

To find out more try contacting your local authorities and local special schools. Charities involved in this area of work are Barnardo's, National Children's Home, NSPCC, Save the Children Fund, ChildLine, Toc H and the Salvation Army.

Working with the disabled

The voluntary agencies which work with the disabled are some of the most progressive. Most of them work on the basis of self-help, and voluntary workers are employed to support disabled people rather than do everything for them. The work more often involves teaching, guidance and social work rather than, for example, cooking or cleaning. People in this field work both in residential homes and clients' own homes. Many disabled people participate in voluntary work themselves.

Jobs in this field are advertised in the local and national press, and the *Community Care* and *Disability Now* journals. Local authorities and hospitals also recruit for this type of work. Some of the voluntary agencies involved include Barnardo's, Leonard Cheshire Foundation, RNID, RNIB, PHAB, Scope, Guide Dogs for the Blind, Mind and Mencap. RADAR is an organisation which coordinates the work of over 500 organisations.

Working with the elderly

Most countries of the world have an increasing elderly population. In many of them government-provided services, where they exist at all, are failing to keep up with the needs of elderly people. This situation is expected to become even more severe in the future. Voluntary agencies have stepped into the gap in many places, and they provide financial help, various practical helping-hand services and even just companionship.

Work with the elderly crosses many different fields. For example, it can involve nursing work, work with the disabled or even work with the poor elderly. Some jobs with elderly people may even involve no work as such, other than just being a companion and a friend to talk to.

Local authorities are a good source of further information. The main charities can also supply details of their work. Help the Aged raises

funds for work with the elderly in the UK and abroad, partly through
its network of charity shops. Age Concern works on practical projects
such as day centres and home visiting. Other large agencies which
work with the elderly include the Anchor Housing Trust, the Sue Ryder
Foundation and the Salvation Army.

Working with the poor

Even in the wealthier countries of the world there are many voluntary
agencies whose aim is to relieve poverty. This is done in a variety of
ways. Some give practical help or money to the poor. Others provide
self-help and education. Others concentrate on raising funds. A number of agencies do not provide direct help, but instead concentrate on
promoting the issues and lobbying governments for more aid or
changes in the law.

For details of opportunities in this type of work contact voluntary
agencies direct. Some of these are CAFOD, Christian Aid, Oxfam, War
on Want, World Vision and the Salvation Army. The Child Poverty
Action Group and Low Pay Unit are agencies which provide information and undertake research and publicity on poverty.

Working on summer camps

In many countries there are summer camps held for children. These
may last for just a week or two, or for the whole summer. Their function is to entertain and care for children, and offer them a range of
activities such as handicrafts, sports and other outdoor pursuits.

There are opportunities to work on these camps in such positions as
monitors, counsellors or even sports instructors (if you are well experienced or qualified in a sport). There are also jobs on the domestic
side, such as catering and odd-jobs staff. Many of these jobs, although
similar to voluntary, are actually on a paid basis.

This type of work can usually only be obtained by applying through
an agency or a company which organises summer camps. This should
be done well in advance of the summer. Such organisations include
PGL, BUNAC and Camp America.

Working on a kibbutz

Spending some time on a kibbutz is not as popular as in the past, but
still an interesting possibility. A kibbutz is a collective farm in Israel.
Many accept volunteers to share the way of life for a time. Food and
basic accommodation is provided free, in return for your labour and
some pay a small pocket-money wage.

The best way to set up a stay on a kibbutz is to use an organisation which can arrange this, such as: Kibbutz Representatives, 1a Accommodation Road, London NW11 8ED. Tel: (020) 8458 9235.

Handy reference
More information about finding voluntary work opportunities abroad, and a comprehensive address listing, can be found in *Doing Voluntary Work Abroad* (How To Books).

CASE HISTORY

Andrew and Bill find voluntary work opens their outlook
Andrew and Bill decided to volunteer for a work camp project during the last three months of their gap year.

'We chose the work camp project partly for charitable reasons and partly because we thought it would be an inexpensive holiday. The latter reason turned out *not* to be a good reason for choosing a work camp, but it all worked out well nevertheless.

'Our project was in a tiny village on the fringe of Snowdonia. Our job was to help restore countryside paths which have been eroded by decades of tourists and walkers. We were in a team of six, working about eight hours a day.

'Our project didn't teach us any skills which we could use in our courses or our careers (transport planning and business studies), but it certainly taught us a lot about organising ourselves and getting on with other people. We both found that it helps us to study problems from all perspectives, rather than just seeing things in black-and-white, which can be a problem with all academic courses.'

CHECKLIST

1. Is voluntary work for you?

2. Would you rather earn a wage?

3. How will voluntary work 'compensate' you, bearing in mind it is not paid?

4. If you're looking to volunteer abroad, is this the best way of travelling abroad?

5. What type of work will you be best suited to?

7
Exchange and Work Experience Opportunities

INVESTIGATING EXCHANGE PROGRAMMES

Is an exchange for you?

An **exchange programme** is an arrangement where you travel abroad to share the home and the lifestyle of someone in a similar position to yourself for a period of weeks or months. In fact, the majority of exchanges do not operate on a reciprocal basis: you can spend some time living with your exchange partner without them necessarily coming back to stay with you.

Finding exchange programmes

Most exchanges are set up as formal arrangements organised by specialist agencies. As such you should make enquiries and applications direct to them. A number of organisations are listed at the end of this book.

For example, a well known organisation called EIL can offer Homestay programmes in a wide range of countries worldwide, for periods of four weeks or longer.

One advantage of following an organised programme is that making an arrangement with a host family, and often travel, will be done at an all-in cost.

You might consider setting up your own exchange programme. To do this you would need to establish contact with someone in another country with a view to arranging an exchange. Ask your school or college if they know of any contacts. Foreign embassies and consulates are also able to offer leads. Penfriend clubs and societies may be used as the basis for setting up an exchange.

LOOKING AT WORK EXPERIENCE

Is work experience for you?

A **work experience** opportunity is similar to an exchange except that, of course, it involves working. This might be for a full year or just a few weeks.

Ideally a work experience scheme should reflect your interests and your future course or career plans. However, this is not strictly essential. If a 'taster' of a given career shows you that it is not right for you then it will have served its purpose well.

Other points to bear in mind when choosing a work experience scheme are:

● the costs involved

● whether the exchange is at home or abroad

● language knowledge required

● and any entry qualifications required.

Finding a work experience opportunity

Most work experience programmes are set up as formal programmes and, as such, you should approach a specialised agency. Some of these are listed later.

The advantage of following an organised programme is that your programme, accommodation and also sometimes travel will be arranged for you, often at an all-in cost. You may, however, find that places are limited. You should normally apply at least three months in advance for such programmes.

Devising your own programme

You can, of course, devise your own work experience programme. This is more practical if you wish to undertake a period of work experience in your own country. Try making written or telephoned approaches to companies in your area.

Some work experience schemes to consider

● The Council on International Educational Exchange (CIEE) has a range of International Internship Programmes which can enable you to spend a period of work experience abroad during a gap year. The range of opportunities for students who are already at university, or who have graduated, is wider still.

● The Army offers short service commissions of up to eighteen months and will consider gap year students. Further details are available from: DAR1d Room 1125, Empress State Building, Lillie Road, London SW6 1TR.

● The International Agricultural Exchange Association can arrange opportunities overseas for those involved in horticulture, agriculture and home management.

● The Year in Industry (YII) can offer paid work experience opportunities with leading companies around the UK. If you are interested in these opportunities you should apply as early as possible in your final A level year at school.

AU PAIRING

Is au pairing for you?

An au pair arrangement is a unique arrangement between an individual and a foreign family. It is not employment as such, but it does allow you to live and work in a foreign country, in a family home, and be paid for it too.

An au pair – who is usually female but male au pairs are accepted in some countries – lives as part of the family. You are not a domestic help. You are not a lodger. Your position is more like that of a sister or brother. Your family provides you with free food and accommodation and a modest pocket-money wage. There may be other benefits, depending on the family. In return you will usually perform such duties as caring for the children, and some housework, for a minimum number of hours each week.

The main purpose of an au pair placement is to allow the au pair to experience life in a foreign country. So every au pair must be given time to pursue personal interests or travel, and many au pairs take language or other classes during their stay.

In the majority of cases au pairing works out very well for both parties. The host family gets a keen, enthusiastic live-in helper. The au pair get to experience a foreign culture at first hand, in a secure environment, and at little or no cost.

Finding a placement

You can use the following methods to find an au pair placement.

UK newspapers

A small number of placements are advertised in the local, regional and national newspapers. In this case you will usually have to apply direct to the host family, either here or abroad.

Magazines

Three magazines which list au pair vacancies are *The Lady*, available every Tuesday at newagents, *Loot*, available in London and some other major cities only, and *Overseas Jobs Express*, available on subscription from: Premier House, Shoreham Airport, BN43 5FF. Tel: (01273) 440220.

Foreign newspapers

Some foreign newspapers are available in the UK and list au pair vacancies as well as many other posts.

An alternative is to place a Situations Wanted advertisement in a foreign newspaper. Try something along the following lines:

CHEERFUL ENGLISH GIRL, 21, seeks au pair position, 6 months.
Driving licence. Contact:

WANT an au pair? British girl, 19, looking for a family.
12 months. France/Germany. Keen. Enthusiastic.
Loves kids and pets. Call:

An advertisement agency can place your ad in foreign newspapers for you:

Frank L. Crane Ltd, 5-15 Cromer Street, London WC1H 8LS. Tel: (020) 7837 3330.

Au pair agencies

A large number of agencies specialise in arranging au pair placements. These agencies are found both in the UK and many other countries and work in different ways. However, their function is basically to register families requiring au pairs, and au pairs requiring placements, then bring them together. They can also help out with contracts, travel, visas and so on. Some agencies are listed later in this book.

Au pair agencies may charge the au pair a fee for arranging a placement. In the UK this is limited by law.

Being a successful au pair

The most difficult part of taking an au pair placement is always the first few days. Your priority, above all the other jobs you have to do, should be to settle yourself in and also to get to know the children you will be looking after.

It is very easy to retreat into a shell in the first few days. Most au pairs worry about whether they have made the right decision at some point in the first few days, so be ready for this. Try to make a positive attempt to become part of the family.

Things to do straight away
Unpack. Settle into your room. Reorganise it, after making sure the family don't mind. Put up posters and any other items you have brought from home. Try to involve the children in this if they are old enough. You'll probably want your room to be fairly private eventually, but it will help to break the ice if you involve them.

Next, make a point of asking the family what you can do to help around the house. But, of course, make sure that whatever you offer to do now you're willing to keep doing for the next year!

What about the 'old' au pair?
Families who take au pairs have often had several, and your predecessor may have departed just a day or two previously.

It is important not to try to copy the methods and routines of the old au pair, which would make things easier initially but is impossible to keep up for a longer period. It can be unsettling for the children while they get used to a new face, but they will probably find it fun too.

Getting the children's trust
It is important to try and get the trust, respect and admiration of the children from the first day. Obviously, if they like you your stay will be much more enjoyable.

It is easy to make the mistake of bribing your way into the children's affections by letting them do things their parents clearly do not allow. Try to resist the temptation, since it will make your job harder and will eventually annoy the parents if they find out.

However, a small gift from your home country will help to break the ice. Other ideas include getting the kids to show you around the house or garden, or even around the local area if they are old enough. This will make them feel needed and liked.

Dealing with reluctant children
This can be a problem sometimes, and most experienced au pairs

reckon the best way to deal with this is to bide your time. Offer your friendship but don't force yourself on the children. Nine times out of ten their reluctance to accept you is down to their routine being disrupted, rather than any dislike of you, and they will come round when things settle down.

What should you do about discipline?
You should make a point of discussing discipline with the parents as soon as you arrive. Remember, parents have widely varying ideas on this and they may differ considerably from what you would do with your own children.

Some parents may be very strict, others quite lax. Some parents will prefer traditional methods, whilst others have very modern ideas. In all cases it is better to try to adopt the parents' views, even if you don't agree with them yourself. For example, many parents, especially in Mediterranean countries such as Italy and Greece, over-indulge their children by British standards. But since the concept of spoiling doesn't exist in these countries there is no point in the au pair trying to reverse the situation.

The main point to establish is whether you are allowed to punish the children. However the safest option nowadays is usually to simply report misbehaviour to the parents.

DO'S AND DON'TS

- Don't retreat into a shell in the first few days.

- Don't idealise home. Think of all the things you can do on your placement that you couldn't do at home.

- Don't wait for the children to make an approach to you.

- Don't indulge the children too much as an easy way to get them to like you.

- Don't pack it all in after the first few days! Even if, in the first few days, you are convinced you have made a mistake, give yourself at least three weeks to settle in before you even think about leaving.

- Do unpack immediately.

- Do get involved straightaway.

- Do sort out the ground rules with the parents straightaway.

- Do involve the children in your settling-in process.

Handy reference
More information on becoming an au pair is available in *Working as an Au Pair* (How To Books).

CASE HISTORY

Chris's work experience takes an unexpected turn
Chris decided to look for work experience during his gap year . . . then found he no longer wanted a 'gap'.

'My original intention was to look for work experience during my gap year – something that would help me in both my university course and my future career. Since these were both to be in the field of accountancy I wrote to all the accountancy firms in my area asking if they had any work experience. Many did not reply, but of those that did one local firm offered to take me on as a general assistant at a salary of £8,000 per year – a fortune to me at the time!

'Although most of the work I did was pretty boring, the job really helped boost my confidence in the world of work. After about six months in the job I applied for a totally different job, as a trainee recruitment consultant, and to my great surprise I got it!

'At the end of my work experience year I decided that I didn't really want to go back to studying, being partly persuaded by the £12,000 salary that my new job offered. Now, three years later, I am still working as a recruitment consultant and have been promoted twice. I have my own flat and car, and a good income, at a time when most people who went to university when I should have done are still looking for their first job and many have large debts to pay off.'

CHECKLIST

1. Is an exchange right for you?

2. Is work experience right for you?

3. Would either foreign travel or voluntary work be more suitable?

8
Arranging Study Opportunities

ADDING TO YOUR QUALIFICATIONS

Deciding to study

Taking some time off to study is not often considered for a gap year, but it can be worthwhile for two reasons:

1. You may be able to add to your qualifications. These are increasingly important in this competitive world when even good A levels, or a good degree do not offer a passport to your chosen career.

2. You will be able to keep up and even develop your study technique. This can be the solution if you are worried, as many gap year students are, that you may find it difficult to get back into an academic routine after your year off.

These are the points you should consider when deciding whether to follow a course of study:

● What would I enjoy? As gap year study is an option it has to be something you really want to do.

● What would be useful to my future course?

● What would be useful to my future career? It is preferable that it is useful, but usefulness to your course is more important.

● What can I afford? There are few options to study free, and some courses are quite expensive.

Another reason for further study might be to improve your A level grades, perhaps if they aren't good enough to get you into your chosen college course. However, since this is really a full time activity it should not be thought of as a gap year as such.

FINDING THE RIGHT COURSE

1. Ask your school or college, since they often know of suitable opportunities.

2. Check with your local colleges and further education institutes. They may have, or know of, opportunities.

3. Look at what courses may be available on a commercial basis. A wide range of exciting commercial courses is now available, covering everything from language study to cookery, although the disadvantage is that you will have to pay the full commercial cost of such courses, which may be high.

4. There are a number of specialist organisations which specialise in arranging study opportunities. The Council on International Educational Exchange (CIEE) can organise study opportunities in Europe, the USA, Canada and other countries worldwide, including languages and other subjects. Their address is given later in the book.

Applying for a course

Once you have decided on a course apply as soon as possible. You must apply for many courses in the spring, prior to their starting date in the autumn.

Gather together evidence of your suitability for the course. For example: relevant subjects being studied, other qualifications, hobbies and interests, future career choices, *etc*.

Gather references and testimonials where these are required. It is often a good idea to ask your school or college for these, before you leave if possible, if there is any possibility that you might want to take a course of study during your gap year. Remember that teachers who know you may have moved on next academic year and, in any case, they will not remember you as well six or ten months on.

Note that, like your college course, some gap year courses of study may only be open to you depending on your A level grades. So always have an alternative in mind if your grades fall slightly short.

Getting help with course fees

You are unlikely to be able to claim any sort of grant as such for gap year study. However, there is a government scheme which effectively offers qualifying students a reduction on fees for certain courses, usually those which lead to an NVQ (National Vocational Qualification). This reduction is currently twenty-four per cent of the course fee.

Ask colleges or training organisations whether their course qualifies for this assistance at the time of looking for a course. If it does you will be asked to fill in a claim form, but the college itself will make the claim for you, leaving you or your parents to pay the remaining seventy-six per cent of the course fee.

GETTING THE MOST FROM FURTHER STUDY

There is an almost unlimited number of subjects you can study. However, in this section we will look at three of the most popular and useful options for gap year study.

Learning a new language

Learning a language can be a good option. It may help your future career and, of course, is a useful skill to possess in any case. If you intend to travel, work or undertake an exchange or study abroad then a language course would be of great assistance.

You could choose a non-vocational course. However, most gap year students opt to study for a language qualification where possible, as this is more likely to impress admission tutors and future employers.

You could take a course with a local further education institute, or a commercial course. However, there are a number of organisations which arrange courses overseas including the Council on International Educational Exchange and organisations such as CESA Languages Abroad. CESA, for example, offers language study programmes lasting from four to six weeks in several European countries, Mexico and the Far East.

Some overseas language courses combine language tuition with a period of travel, work experience, an exchange scheme or voluntary work.

Learning a trade or vocational skill

Some gap year students opt to learn a trade or vocational skill. Apart from the general interest aspect this can be useful as a second career, to fall back on in the future. If you take a short course you may be able to use it to find a suitable job later on in your gap year.

There are many subjects to choose from, both vocational and non-vocational. Options include:

● secretarial courses

● computing courses

● catering/cooking

● acting

● modelling

● music.

To find out about these courses try your local authority colleges and local privately-run colleges.

Learning a sport

If you are interested in a particular sport then a course of study during your gap year might allow you not only to enjoy and develop your sport, but gain a qualification in it too. One variation on this idea is to study for a qualification at the start of the gap year, then use it to find employment as an instructor later on in your year off, for example in a summer holiday resort, a ski resort or a children's camp.

If you are interested in taking a sporting course, you can normally obtain details of approved courses which lead to a recognised qualification from the professional organisation which represents that sport. Note that some sporting courses are for enjoyment only and will not qualify you to teach.

Studying abroad

One possibility you might consider is to study abroad, at a foreign university or college. This may not only provide further useful qualifications, but will also help you develop your personal and study skills.

Foreign study, however, should not be undertaken lightly. It is difficult enough to study something well at home, let alone in a foreign country. If you were to study in a country where English is not spoken you would also need to speak and write the relevant language to an acceptable standard.

There is also the cost to consider. Not only will there be tuition fees to pay, but also living costs. You may be able to get a grant or sponsorship, although the chances are fairly slim.

To find out about courses ask your school or college. The Council on International Educational Exchange also offers foreign study programmes in a variety of subjects. The Fullbright Commission offers information on study opportunities in the USA.

USEFUL INFORMATION

Visas and permits

You will probably need a visa or permit to study in any foreign country. This should normally be obtained from the embassy or consulate of the country concerned before leaving for your period of study. Although in most countries, such as the USA, visas to enable you to follow an approved course of study are often quite readily granted, they do not usually allow you to work as well.

The main exception to this rule is nationals of one EU country wishing to study in another. You will not need a visa or any sort of permit to enter. However, you will require a residence permit if you stay for more than three months. This can be obtained after you have arrived.

Comparability of foreign qualifications

Always check whether the qualifications you will obtain from studying abroad is comparable with, and acceptable alongside, similar qualifications at home. If it is not it may be of little value to you once you return home.

In fact foreign qualifications are *not* usually officially comparable with those in other countries. The main exception is qualifications issued within the EU. Here, most qualifications in similar subjects involving a similar level of knowledge will eventually be regarded as officially comparable throughout the EU, but this process is taking time to implement. For example, degree-level qualifications are theoretically regarded as comparable throughout the UK, but the level to which other qualifications are comparable varies from industry to industry.

You can find out whether your intended qualification is likely to be considered officially comparable to any similar UK qualification from:

The Comparability Co-Ordinator, Employment Department, Qualifications and Standards Branch-QSI, Room E454, Moorfoot, Sheffield S1 4PQ. Tel: (0141) 259 4144.

You can also obtain information on this from:

Commission of the European Communities, Jean Monnet House, Storey's Gate, London SW1P 3AT. Tel: (020) 7973 1992.

CASE HISTORY

Anne's studies are enjoyable as well as valuable

Anne decided to spend some of her gap year studying French.

'Although I had obtained a good GCSE in French I never thought of French as being one of my strongest subjects. I decided to study it in my gap year partly because I thought it would help with my future career, but also to help me keep up the study habit.

'My programme of study was organised by a commercial language school. The programme cost almost £800 and fortunately my parents offered to help me with some of the cost. The programme consisted of organised lessons every morning, with a range of optional social activities in the afternoons and evenings. I stayed with a local family in Grenoble, which was one of the most enjoyable parts of the whole experience.

'In response to the question as to whether I found the course helpful the answer is most definitely yes. I am now almost fluent – in spoken French at least – and feel a lot more confident, too. I think my gap year experience will certainly be of use to me in my future career, which I hope will be in international marketing.'

CHECKLIST

1. Do you *need* any more qualifications?

2. Do you *want* any more qualifications?

3. What would you like to study?

4. What will benefit you most?

9
Summing Up

This book has shown you just what an exciting and diverse range of opportunities is available to you in a gap year. There are so many things to do, and places to go, that no book can cover absolutely everything, but we hope we have given you a taste of the opportunities.

You might not, of course, have found anything that appeals to you for your gap year. If so, it may be because a gap year isn't for you, and that you'd rather press on and get started at college. It may alternatively be that none of the traditional gap year activities appeals to you. If so, then go out and find something that you *do* want to do. There are absolutely no restrictions on what a gap year should consist of!

PLANNING FOR ANYTHING BUT A GAP

But whatever you choose to do, make sure that you plan it. Planning may seem boring at the time, but it will make all the difference. If you follow the general principle that a gap year should enhance your future prospects and not merely mark time, or even damage those prospects, you will not go far wrong.

Your gap year is your year to do what you want to do. As such it can consist of anything, but it should be *anything but a gap*!

TEN MORE TIPS FOR A SUCCESSFUL YEAR

To make the most of your year:

- Get started/leave as soon as your exams have finished.

- If you want a holiday, have one. When it's over move on to something else. Your year shouldn't be one long holiday!

- Plan something to look forward to for the end.

Gap Year Planner

June (A levels end) ....

July..

August ....

September ....

October ....

November ....

December..

January..

February...

March...

April..

May ....

June ....

July..

August ....

September (new academic year starts) ....

Fig. 10. Planning your gap year.

- Autumn is a good time for working; there are more seasonal jobs in the pre-Christmas rush.

- There is a very limited choice of things to do in January-March. Think ahead carefully.

- Be really sure about your course and have everything sorted out before your gap year. It is more difficult and time-consuming to see to this once you are away from school or college.

- If there is something you really want to do, do it.

- Always have contingency plans for if things go wrong.

- Sort out the money side early on. Don't just hope you'll be able to afford it.

- Don't plan to take your entire gap year with someone else; it is unlikely to run smoothly.

Useful Addresses

This section gives the addresses of companies and other organisations which may be of assistance in starting to plan a gap year.

TRAVEL AND ACCOMMODATION CONTACTS

Association of British Travel Agents (ABTA), 55 Newman Street, London W1P 4AH. Tel: (020) 7637 2444.

Camping and Caravanning Club, Green Fields House, Westwood Way, Coventry CV4 8SH. Information and advice for campers. Issues Camping Carnets.

Campus Travel, 52 Grosvenor Gardens, London SW1W 0AG. Tel: (020) 7730 3402. Discount travel agency.

Council Travel, 28a Poland Street, London W1V 3DB. Tel: (020) 7287 3337. Discount travel agency.

Eurolines, 4 Cardiff Road, Luton LU1 1PP. Tel: (01582) 456654. Europe-wide coach operator.

Passport offices

Clive House, 70-78 Petty France, London SW1H 9HD.

Fifth Floor, India Buildings, Water Street, Liverpool L2 0QZ.

Olympia House, Upper Dock Street, Newport, Gwent NP9 1XA.

Aragon Court, Northminster Road, Peterborough PE1 1QC.

3 Northgate, 96 Milton Street, Cowcaddens, Glasgow G4 0BT.

Hampton House, 47-53 High Street, Belfast BT1 2QS.

Telephone numbers of all passport offices is 0870 5210410.

Rapid Visa Service, 131-135 Earls Court Road, London SW5 9RH. Tel: (020) 7373 3026.

Scottish Youth Hostel Association, 7 Glebe Crescent, Stirling FK8 2JA. Tel: (01786) 451181.

STA Travel, 6 Wrights Lane, London W8 6TA. Tel: (020) 7938 4711. Discount travel agency.

Thames Consular Services, 548 Chiswick High Road, London W4 4HS. Tel: (020) 8995 2492. Can obtain visas on behalf of travellers.

Thomas Cook Passport and Visa Service, 45 Berkeley Street, London W1A 1EB. Tel: (020) 7408 4141. Can obtain visas on behalf of travellers.

Trailfinders, 42/50 Earls Court Road, London W8 6EJ. Tel: (020) 7938 3366. Discount travel agency.

Travelmates, 15 Cavendish Road, Bournemouth BH7 7AD. Tel: (01202) 558314. Introduction service for lone travellers.

WEXAS International, 45-49 Brompton Road, London SW3 1DE. Tel: (020) 7589 3315. Discount travel services.

Youth Hostels Association (England & Wales), 8 St Stephen's Hill, St Albans, Herts AL1 2DY. Tel: (01727) 55215.

EMPLOYMENT AGENCIES

Selected agencies in EU countries.

Austria
National employment service
Bebenbergerstrasse 33, 8021 Graz.
Schopfstrasse 5, Innsbruck.
Schiesstantstrasse 4, 5021 Salzburg.
Hohenstauffengasse 2, 1013 Vienna.
Weihburggasse 30, Vienna.

Belgium

National employment service
Offices in most towns.
Flanders: VDAB.
Wallonia: ONEM.

Private employment agencies
ECCO, 17a Rue Vilian XIV, 1050 Brussels. Tel: 02 647 87 80.
Avenue Louise Interim, 207 Avenue Louise, 1050 Brussels. Tel: 02 640 91 91.
Select Interim, 1-5 Avenue de la Joyeuse Entrée, 1040 Brussels. Tel: 02 231 03 33.
Creyf's, 473 Avenue Louise, 1050 Brussels. Tel: 02 646 34 34.

Denmark

National employment service
Arbejdsformidlingen, Adelgade 13, Copenhagen 1304.

Finland

National employment service
Ministry of Labour, Fabianinkatu 32, 00100 Helsinki 10.

France

National employment service
ANPE, 92136 Issy les Moulineaux, Paris, and offices in all towns.

Private employment agencies
ECCO, 33 Rue Raffet, 75016 Paris. Tel: 1 45 25 51 51.
Kelly, 50 Avenue des Champs Elysees, 75008 Paris. Tel: 1 42 56 44 88.
Manpower, 9 Rue Jacques Bingen, 75017 Paris. Tel: 1 47 66 03 03.

Germany

National employment service
Arbeitsamt. Offices in all towns.
ZAV, Feuerbachstrasse 42, 6000 Frankfurt Am Main.
If applying from outside Germany.

Greece

National employment service
OAED, Thakris 8, 16610 Glyfada, Athens. Tel: 01 993 2589.

Private employment agencies
Athenian Agency, PO Box 51181, TK 14510 Kiffissia, Athens. Tel: 301 808 1005.
Camenos International Staff Consultancy, 12 Botsai Street, Athens 147.
Intertom Agency, 24-26 Halkokondili Street, Athens 10432. Tel: 01 532 9470.
Pioneer, 11 Nikis Street, Athens 10557. Tel: 01 322 4321.

Ireland

National employment service
FÁS, 65a Adelaide Road, Dublin 2. Tel: 01 765861. Also has local offices in most towns.

Italy

National employment service
Ufficio di Collocamento, Mandopera, Via Pastrengo 16, Rome.

Luxembourg

National employment service
38a Rue Philippe II, 2340 Luxembourg. Tel: 478 5300.

Netherlands

National employment service
Singel 202, 1016 AA Amsterdam. Tel: 020 520 0911.
Begynenhof 8, 5611 EL Eindhoven. Tel: 040 325325.
Engelse Kamp 4, 9722 AX Groningen. Tel: 050 225911.
Troelstrakade 65, 2531 AA The Hague.
Schiedamse Vest 160, 3011 BH Rotterdam.

Private employment agencies
Manpower, Van Baerlestraat 16, Amsterdam.

Portugal

National employment service
Ministério de Trabalho, Praça de Londres, 1091 Lisbon, Codex.

Spain

National employment service
Instituto Nacional de Empleo (INEM), General Pardinas 5, Madrid.

Sweden

National employment service
Arbetmarknadsstryrelsen, Box 2021, 12612 Stockholm.

United Kingdom

National employment service
Job Centres. In most towns.

VOLUNTARY WORK AGENCIES AND CHARITIES

Age Concern England, 1268 London Road, London SW16 4ER. Tel:
(020) 8679 8000.
ATD Fourth World, 48 Addington Street, London SE5 7LB. Tel: (020)
7703 3231.
Barnardo's, Tanner's Lane, Barkingside, Ilford, Essex IG6 1QG.
British Red Cross Society, 9 Grosvenor Crescent, London SW1X 7EJ.
Tel: (020) 7235 5454.
British Trust for Conservation Volunteers (BTCV), 36 St Mary's

Street, Wallingford, Oxfordshire OX10 0EU. Tel: (01491) 839766.

CAFOD, Romero Close, Stockwell Road, London SW9 9TY. Tel: (020) 7733 7900.

Cancer Research, 6-10 Cambridge Crescent, London NW1Y 4JL. Tel: (020) 7224 1333.

ChildLine, Royal Mail Building, Studd Street, London N1 0QW. Tel: (020) 7239 1000.

Christian Aid, 35 Lower Marsh, London SE1 6RL. Tel: (020) 7620 4444.

Christian Movement for Peace, 186 St Paul's Road, Birmingham B12 8LZ. Tel: (0121) 446 5704.

Christians Abroad, 1 Stockwell Green, London SW9 9HP. Tel: (020) 7737 7811.

Community Service Volunteers, 237 Pentonville Road, London N1 9NJ. Tel: (020) 7278 6601.

Council for the Protection of Rural England, Warwick House, Buckingham Palace Road, London SW1W 0PP. Tel: (020) 7976 6433.

Friends of the Earth, 26-28 Underwood Street, London N1 7JQ. Tel: (020) 7490 1555.

Greenpeace, Canonbury Villas, London N1 2PN. Tel: (020) 7354 5100.

Help the Aged, St James Walk, London EC1R 0BE. Tel: (020) 7253 0253.

Imperial Cancer Research Fund, PO Box 123, London WC2A 3PX. Tel: (020) 7242 0200.

International Voluntary Service (IVS), Old Hall, East Bergholt, Colchester CO7 6TQ. Tel: (01206) 298215.

National Association of Citizens Advice Bureaux (NACAB), 115-123 Pentonville Road, London N1 9LZ. Tel: (020) 7833 2181.

National Children's Home (NCH), 85 Highbury Park, London N5 1UD. Tel: (020) 7226 2033.

National Trust, 36 Queen Anne's Gate. London SW1H 9AS. Tel: (020) 7222 9251.

Oxfam, 274 Banbury Road, Oxford OX2 7DZ. Tel: (01865) 311311.

Royal National Institute for the Deaf (RNID), 105 Gower Street, London WC1E 6AH. Tel: (020) 7387 8033.

Royal National Institute for the Blind (RNIB), 224 Great Portland Street, London W1N 6AA. Tel: (020) 7388 1266.

Royal Society for the Prevention of Cruelty to Animals (RSPCA), The Causeway, Horsham, Sussex RH12 1HG. Tel: (01403) 64181.

Royal Society for the Protection of Birds (RSPB), The Lodge, Sandy, Bedfordshire SG19 2DL. Tel: (01767) 680551.

Salvation Army, 101 Queen Victoria Street, London EC4P 4EP. Tel: (020) 7236 5222.

Save the Children Fund, 17 Grove Lane, London SE5 8RD. Tel: (020) 7703 5400.

Scope, 12 Park Crescent, London W1N 4EQ. Tel: (020) 7636 5020.

United Nations Association (Wales), International Youth Service, Temple of Peace, Cathays Park, Cardiff CF1 3AP. Tel: (029) 20223088.

EXCHANGE AND WORK EXPERIENCE OPPORTUNITIES

BUNAC (British Universities North America Club), 16 Bowling Green Lane, London EC1R 0BD. Tel: (020) 7251 3472. Offers opportunities in summer camps, and can also arrange visas for casual work in the USA, Canada and Australia.

Camp America, 37a Queens Gate, London SW7 5HR. Tel: (020) 7581 7373. Offers opportunities in summer camps in the USA.

Council on International Educational Exchange (CIEE), 52 Poland Street, London W1V 4JQ. Tel: (020) 7478 2007. Offers several international work experience programmes.

EIL Ltd, 287 Worcester Road, Malvern WR14 1AB. Tel: (01684) 563577. Offers homestay and au pair programmes worldwide.

Fill the Gap, World Challenge, Black Arrow House, 2 Chandos Road, London NW10 6NF. Tel: (020) 8961 1122. Can offer work and voluntary work worldwide.

GAP Activity Projects, GAP House, 44 Queen's Road, Reading RG1 4BB. Tel: (0118) 6594914. Offers gap year work/voluntary work projects.

Kibbutz Representatives, 1a Accommodation Road, London NW11 8ED. Tel: (020) 8458 9235. Arranges stays on a kibbutz.

PGL, Alton Court, Penyard Lane, Ross on Wye, Herefordshire HR9 5NR. Tel: (01989) 764211. PGL is not a work experience organisation but does employ leaders/instructors for its children's camps.

Raleigh International, Raleigh House, 27 Parson's Green Lane, London SW6 4HZ. Tel: (020) 7371 8585. Organises expeditions, rather than work experience/exchanges as such.

The Army (Short Service Commissions), DAR1d Room 1125, Empress State Building, Lillie Road, London SW6 1TR. Short service commissions, suitable for a gap year.

AU PAIR AGENCIES

Aaron Employment Agency, The Courtyard, Stanley Road, Tunbridge Wells, Kent TN1 2RJ. Tel: (01892) 546601.

Abbey Au Pairs, 8 Boulnois Avenue, Parkstone, Poole, Dorset BH14 9NX. Tel: (01202) 732922.

Academy Au Pair and Nanny Agency Ltd, Glenlea, Dulwich Common, London SE21 7ES. Tel: (020) 8299 4599.

Au Pair in America, 37 Queen's Gate, London SW7 5HR. Tel: (020) 7581 7322.

Avalon Au Pairs, 7 Highway, Edgcumbe Park, Crowthorne, Berkshire. Tel: (01344) 778246.

Bingham Placements, 9 Bingham Place, London W1M 3FH. Tel: (020) 7224 4016.

Delaney International, Middleton Lodge, Munstead Park, Godalming, Surrey GU8 4AR. Tel: (01483) 424343.

Euro Employment Centre, 42 Upper Union Arcade, Bury, Lancs BL9 0QF. Tel: (0161) 797 6400.

Euro Pair Agency, 28 Derwent Avenue, Pinner, Middlesex HA5 4QJ. Tel: (020) 8421 2100.

EIL Ltd, 287 Worcester Road, Malvern WR14 1AB. Tel: (01684) 563577.

HCA Anglia, 154 Fronks Road, Dovercourt, Essex CO12 4EF. Tel: (01255) 503717.

Janet White Employment Agency, 67 Jackson Avenue, Leeds LS8 1NS. Tel: (0113) 266 6507.

Jolaine Au Pair and Domestic Agency, 18 Escot Way, Barnet, Hertfordshire EN5 3AN. Tel: (020) 8449 1334.

Kensington and Chelsea Nurses and Nannies, 168 Sloane Street, London SW1X 9QF. Tel: (020) 7581 5454.

North South Agency, 28 Wellington Road, Hastings, East Sussex TN34 3RN. Tel: (01424) 422364.

Simply Domestics, 103 Cranley Gardens, London N10 3AD. Tel: (020) 8444 4303.

South Eastern Au Pair Bureau, 39 Rutland Avenue, Thorpe Bay, Essex SS1 2XJ. Tel: (01702) 601911.

Universal Care Ltd, Chester House, 9 Windsor Road, Beaconsfield, Buckinghamshire HP9 2JJ. Tel: (01494) 678811.

COLLEGES AND STUDY ORGANISATIONS

CESA Languages Abroad, Western House, Malpas, Truro TR1 1SQ. Tel: (01872) 225300. Offers language courses abroad.

Council on International Educational Exchange (CIEE), 52 Poland Street, London W1V 4JQ. Tel: (020) 7478 2007. Offers several international language study programmes.

Fulbright Commission, 62 Doughty Street, London WC1N 2LS. Tel: (020) 7404 6994. Information on study at US universities.

International Agricultural Exchange Association, YFC Centre, NAC, Stoneleigh Park, Kenilworth, Warwickshire CV8 2LG. Tel: (024) 76696578. Work experience and exchange scheme for agricultural students.

MISCELLANEOUS USEFUL ADDRESSES

Berlitz School of Languages, Wells House, 79 Wells Street, London W1A 3BZ. Tel: (020) 7580 6482. Language classes and courses.

British Airways Immunisation Service, 101 Cheapside, London EC2. Tel: (020) 7606 2977. No appointment necessary for immunisations, BA Travel Clinics are also in twenty-five other towns.

Commission of the European Communities, Jean Monnet House, Storey's Gate, London SW1P 3AT. Tel: (020) 7973 1992. Information on comparability of qualifications.

Comparability Co-Ordinator, Employment Department, Qualifications and Standards Branch-QSI, Room E454, Moorfoot, Sheffield S1 4PQ. Tel: (020) 7210 4850. Information on comparability of qualifications.

Department of Health, Public Enquiries Office, Richmond House, 79 Whitehall, London SW1A 2NS. Tel: (020) 7210 4850. Information on health services.

Department of Social Security, Overseas Branch, Newcastle Upon Tyne NE98 1YX. Can provide information on availability of health services in Europe. Call (0800) 555777 for leaflets.

Frank L. Crane Ltd, 5-15 Cromer Street, London WC1II 8LS. Tel: (020) 7837 3330. Advertisement agency for foreign newspapers.

HM Customs Advice Centre, Dorset House, Stamford Street, London SE1 9NG. Tel: (020) 7202 4227. Advice on customs regulations in the UK.

ISIC Mail Order, Bleaklow House, Mill Street, Glossop, Derbyshire SK13 8PT. Tel: (01203) 694995. Issues ISIC discount card, entitling students to discounts on travel, accommodation and other purchases.

Linguaphone, St Giles House, 50 Poland Street, London W1V 4AX. Tel: (020) 7734 0574. Provides language courses.

Medical Advisory Service for Travellers Abroad (MASTA), Keppel Street, London WC1E 7HT. Tel: (0891) 224100. Provides a premium rate telephone hotline for travel medical queries.

National Association of Volunteer Bureaux, New Oxford House, Waterloo Street, Birmingham B2 5UG. Tel: (0121) 633 4555. Contacts with local volunteer bureaux in your area.

NCVO News, Regent's Wharf, 8 All Saints Street, London N1 9RL. Tel: (020) 7713 6161. News and information for those working for voluntary agencies.

Overseas Jobs Express, Premier House, Shoreham Airport, Sussex BN43 5FF. Tel: (01273) 440220. Newspaper with overseas job vacancy advertisements.

Royal Society of Arts, Westwood Way, Coventry CV4 8HS. Tel: (024) 7647 0033. Offers TEFLA qualification, amongst many others.

Stanfords, 12-14 Long Acre, London WC2 9LP. Tel: (020) 7836 1321. Reputedly the largest map seller in the world. Offers a mail order service.

The Lady, 39-40 Bedford Street, London WC2E 9ER. Tel: (020) 7379 4717.

The Year in Industry (YII), University of Manchester, Simon Building, Oxford Road, Manchester M13 9PL. Tel: (0161) 275 4396. Can offer paid gap year placements in industry.

Universities and Colleges Admissions Service, (UCAS), PO Box 67, Cheltenham, Gloucestershire GL50 3SF. Tel: (01242) 227788.

Volunteer Centre UK, 29 Lower King's Road, Berkhamsted, Hertfordshire HP4 2AB. Tel: (01442) 873311. Contacts with voluntary projects in your area.

EMBASSIES AND CONSULATES

Australia
The Strand, London WC2B 2LA. Tel: (020) 7379 4334.

Austria
18 Belgrave Mews West, London SW1X 8HU. Tel: (020) 7235 3731.

Baltic States

Estonia
16 Hyde Park Gate, London SW7 5DG. Tel: (020) 7589 3428.

Latvia
72 Queensborough Terrace, London W2 3SP. Tel: (020) 7727 1698.

Lithuania
17 Essex Villas, London W8 7BP. Tel: (020) 7938 2481.

Belgium
103 Eaton Square, London SW1W 9AB. Tel: (020) 7235 5422.

Brazil
32 Green Street, London W1Y 3FD. Tel: (020) 7499 0877.

Bulgaria
186 Queen's Gate, London SW7 3HL. Tel: (020) 7584 9400.

Canada
1 Grosvenor Square, London W1X 0AB. Tel: (020) 7629 9492.

Chile
12 Devonshire Street, London W1N 2DS. Tel: (020) 7580 6392.

China
49 Portland Place, London W1N 3AH.

Czech Republic
25 Kensington Palace Gardens, London W8 4QX. Tel: (020) 7229 1255.

Denmark
55 Sloane Street, London SW1X 9SR. Tel: (020) 7235 1255.

Egypt
26 South Street, London W1Y 8EL. Tel: (020) 7499 2401.

Finland
38 Chesham Place, London SW1X 8HW. Tel: (020) 7235 9531.

France
58 Knightsbridge, London SW1X 7JT. Tel: (020) 7235 8080.

Germany
23 Belgrave Square, London SW1X 8PZ. Tel: (020) 7235 5033.

Greece
1a Holland Park, London W11 3TP. Tel: (020) 7727 8040.

Hungary
35 Eaton Place, London SW1. Tel: (020) 7235 4048.

India
India House, Aldwych, London WC2B 4NA. Tel: (020) 7836 8484.

Ireland
17 Grosvenor Place, London SW1X 7HR. Tel: (020) 7235 2171.

Israel
2 Palace Green, London W8 4QB. Tel: (020) 7937 8050.

Italy
14 Three Kings Yard, London W1Y 2EH. Tel: (020) 7629 8200.

Japan
46 Grosvenor Street, London W1X 0BA. Tel: (020) 7493 6030.

Luxembourg
27 Wilton Crescent, London SW1X 8SD. Tel: (020) 7235 6961.

Malaysia
45 Belgrave Square, London SW1X 8QT. Tel: (020) 7235 8033.

Mexico
8 Halkin Street, London SW1 0AR. Tel: (020) 7235 6393.

Netherlands
38 Hyde Park Gate, London SW7 5DP. Tel: (020) 7581 5040.

New Zealand
New Zealand House, London SW1Y 4TQ.

Norway
25 Belgrave Square, London SW1X 8QD. Tel: (020) 7235 7151.

Peru
52 Sloane Street, London SW1X 9SP. Tel: (020) 7235 1917.

Poland
47 Portland Place, London W1N 3AG. Tel: (020) 7580 4324.

Portugal
62 Brompton Road, London SW3 1BJ. Tel: (020) 7581 8722.

Romania
4 Palace Green, London W8 4QD. Tel: (020) 7937 9666.

Russia
13 Kensington Palace Gardens, London W8 4QX. Tel: (020) 7229 3628.

Slovak Republic
25 Kensington Palace Gardens, London W8 4QY. Tel: (020) 7243
0803.

Singapore
2 Wilton Crescent, London SW1X 8RW. Tel: (020) 7235 8315.

Spain
24 Belgrave Square, London SW1X 8QA. Tel: (020) 7235 5555.

Sweden
11 Montagu Place, London W1H 2AL. Tel: (020) 7724 2101.

Switzerland
16-18 Montagu Place, London W1H 2BQ. Tel: (020) 7723 0701.

Thailand
29-30 Queen's Gate, London SW7 5JB. Tel: (020) 7589 2944.

Turkey
43 Belgrave Square, London SW1X 8AP. Tel: (020) 7235 5252.

United States of America
24-32 Grosvenor Sqaure, London W1A 1AE. Tel: (020) 7499 9000.

(Representatives of Commonwealth countries are known as High
Commissions.)

Further Reading

Applying for a Job, Judith Johnstone (How To Books).
Backpacking Round Europe, Mark Hempshell (How To Books).
Budget Guide to Europe, (Let's Go).
Cheap Eats Guide to Europe, (Harper Collins).
Cheap Sleep Guide to Europe, (Harper Collins).
Doing Voluntary Work Abroad, Mark Hempshell (How To Books).
Europe: The Rough Guide (Harrap Columbus).
Finding a Job in Computers, Stephen Harding (How To Books).
Getting a Job in Australia, Nick Vandome (How To Books).
Getting a Job in Travel and Tourism, Mark Hempshell (How To Books).
Getting That Job, Joan Fletcher (How To Books).
Hitchhikers' Guide to Europe (Harper Collins).
Hostelling International (IYHA).
How to Find Temporary Work Abroad, Nick Vandome (How To Books).
How to Master Languages, Roger Jones (How To Books).
How to Work in an Office, Sheila Payne (How To Books).
How to Work in Retail, Sylvia Lichfield and Christine Hall (How To Books).
International Travel Health Guide, Stuart R. Rose (Travel Medicine).
Living and Working in Australia, Laura Veltman (How To Books).
Nothing Ventured: Disabled people travel the world (Rough Guides).
Overseas Timetable: Railways, road and shipping (Thomas Cook).
Spending a Year Abroad, Nick Vandome (How To Books).
Travel Around the World, Nick Vandome (How To Books).
The Traveller's Handbook (Wexas Ltd).
Traveller's Health: How to stay healthy abroad (Oxford University Press).
Women Travel (Rough Guides).
Working Holidays Abroad, Mark Hempshell (Kuperard).
Working in Hotels and Catering, Mark Hempshell (How To Books).

Index

STUDYING AT UNIVERSITY
How to make a success of your academic course

Kevin Bucknall

University life is wonderful and exciting but many students at first find it mysterious and a little frightening. It can be hard to adjust to the high degree of academic freedom. This book will help to banish any fears by explaining how to adapt to the pressures of your new course. You will learn what is expected of you and how to meet these demands week by week. The skills you need are best learned early in your first year but they will be constantly used during the whole of your time at university. These skills include taking notes, finding information, and then using it effectively in essays, orals and exams. Dr Kevin Bucknall has over 30 years' experience in university teaching in England and Australia. He presently teaches economics to first year students.

136pp illus. 1 85703 219 5.

GETTING A JOB ABROAD
The handbook for the international jobseeker; where the jobs are, how to get them

Roger Jones

Now in a fifth fully revised edition, this top-selling title is essential for everyone planning to spend a period abroad. It contains a big reference section of medium and long-term job opportunities and possibilities, arranged by region and country of the world, and by profession/ occupation. There is a classified guide to overseas recruitment agencies, and even a multi-lingual guide to writing application letters. 'A fine book for anyone considering even a temporary overseas job.' *The Evening Star.* 'A highly informative and well researched book . . . containing lots of hard information and a first class reference section . . . A superb buy.' *The Escape Committee Newsletter.* 'A valuable addition to any careers library.' *Phoenix (Association of Graduate Careers Advisory Services).* 'An excellent addition to any careers library . . . Compact and realistic . . . There is a wide range of reference addresses covering employment agencies, specialist newspapers, a comprehensive booklist and helpful addresses . . . All readers, whether careers officers, young adults or more mature adults, will find use for this book.' *Newscheck/Careers Services Bulletin.* Roger Jones has himself worked abroad for many years and is a specialist writer on expatriate and employment matters.

336pp illus. 1 85703 418 X. 5th edition.

GETTING A JOB IN TRAVEL & TOURISM
Where to find the best jobs and how to secure them

Mark Hempshell

Would you enjoy working in travel and tourism? Do you already have a local position, but want to venture overseas? Whatever your age, background or qualifications, this book will open doors for you. With lots of examples, it shows how and where to obtain really great jobs as couriers, holiday reps, coach drivers, tour guides, entertainers, sports instructors or airline staff. Or how about working on cruise ships, in top hotels and restaurants, on safaris, summer camps, winter sports or other exotic assignments? The book tells you what each job involves, the skills, qualifications, experience, language, training, permits, pay and conditions – plus where to find the vacancies and how to apply. Someone has to do all these glamorous jobs – use this book, and it could be you! Mark Hempshell's other books include *Your Own Business in Europe, Working in Hotels & Catering, Getting a Job in Europe, How to Get a Job in France* and others in this series.

176pp illus. 1 85703 268 3. 3rd edition.

STUDYING FOR A DEGREE
How to succeed as a mature student in higher education

Stephen Wade

If you are an aspiring student in adult education, or a mature learner looking for a higher education course leading to a degree, this book is specially for you. It will lead you through the academic maze of entry procedures, study programmes and teaching methods. It explains how to apply and how to contact the professionals who will help; how to survive tutorials, seminars and presentations, and how to manage your time, plan your study, and find the right support when you need it. There are sections on the credit award system, pathway planning, and useful case studies of typical students in this context. Stephen Wade PhD has 20 years' professional experience in further and higher education, and is a Course Leader for a degree programme.

128pp illus. 1 85703 415 5.

HOW TO STUDY & LEARN
Your practical guide to effective study skills

Peter Marshall

Are you thinking of studying or training for an important qualification? Do you know the right techniques for studying and learning, to ensure you achieve the best results as quickly as possible? Whether you are at college or university, doing projects and assignments, writing essays, receiving continuous assessment or preparing for exams, this is the book for you. In practical steps it covers getting your thinking right, organising yourself properly, finding and processing the information you need, reading effectively, developing good writing skills, thinking creatively, motivating yourself, and more. Whatever your subject, age or background, start now – and turn yourself into a winning candidate. Peter Marshall BA BSc (Econ) has a wealth of experience as a university and college teacher.

144pp illus. 1 85703 435 X. 2nd edition.

PASSING THAT INTERVIEW
Your step-by-step guide to achieving success

Judith Johnstone

Everyone knows how to shine at interview – or do they? When every candidate becomes the perfect clone of the one before, you have to have that extra 'something' to raise your chances above the rest. Using a systematic and practical approach, this **How To** book takes you step-by-step through the essential pre-interview groundwork, the interview encounter itself, and what you can learn from the experience afterwards. The book contains sample pre- and post-interview correspondence, and is complete with a guide to further reading, glossary of terms, and index. 'This is from the first class How To Books stable.' *Escape Committee Newsletter*. 'Offers a fresh approach to a well documented subject.' *Newscheck/Careers Service Bulletin*. 'A complete step-by-step guide.' *The Association of Business Executives*. Judith Johnstone is a Graduate of the Institute of Personnel & Development; she has been an instructor in Business Studies and adult literacy tutor, and has long experience of helping people at work.

144pp illus. 1 85703 538 0. 5th edition.

FINDING A JOB WITH A FUTURE
How to identify and work in growth industries and services

Laurel Alexander

Are you seeking to change your career? Have you been made redundant? Are you returning to work? If you want to ensure a long lasting career move in the right direction, you need to read this book which sets out in a practical way, growth areas of industry and commerce. Discover the work cycle of the future based on job specific skills, abstract skills, continuous learning and life-time career planning. Learn about flexible ways of working. There is occupational information on IT, training and education, business services, leisure, the entertainment industry, social and cultural fields, security and protective services, science and working for the environment. There are job and personal self assessments for each section, plus where to go for training and how to find the jobs. Laurel Alexander is a manager/trainer in career development who has helped many individuals succeed in changing their work direction.

144pp illus. 1 85703 310 8.

RESEARCH METHODS
How to design and conduct a successful project

Peter Marshall

Research can do as much to mislead as to enlighten if not done competently. This book seeks to present the various methods available to social researchers, explain the basic principles and discuss some of their strengths and weaknesses. It deals with both the rigorous quantitative methods of those purely concerned with explanation, and the less rigorous qualitative methods of those more interested in understanding than explaining. It also gives guidance on building complementary methods into research designs. Whether you are new to the subject, or an established practitioner who needs a straightforward handbook to refer to, or teach from, this book should prove valuable. Dr Marshall is a member of The Applied Psychology Research Group of Royal Holloway, University of London. He is also an experienced university and college teacher.

120pp illus. 1 85703 410 4.

GETTING YOUR FIRST JOB
How to win the offer of good prospects and a regular pay packet

Penny Hitchin

It's a tough world for jobhunters – especially for those with no track record. The days when newcomers to the job market could walk into 'A job for life' have gone. Jobseekers today must impress a potential employer with their personal qualities and attitudes as well as their paper qualifications. Once in work, they must show themselves to be willing, adaptable and flexible – able to learn new skills quickly and cope with constant change. This readable handbook offers young people a real insight into what employers are looking for, encouraging the reader to take a constructive and positive approach to finding their first job. The book includes lots of practical examples, self-assessment material and typical case studies. Penny Hitchin has run Jobfinder programmes and written careers books and materials for TV and radio campaigns on training and employment.

128pp illus. 1 85703 300 0.

HOW TO GET A JOB IN EUROPE
A guide to employment opportunities and contacts

Mark Hempshell

Europe's rise as the world's leading economic unit has made it *the* place to get a job. This book sets out exactly what opportunities exist in Europe. It will be an absolutely essential starting point for everyone job-hunting in Europe, whether as a school or college leaver, graduate trainee, technician or professional – and indeed anyone wanting to live and work as a European whether for just a summer vacation or on a more permanent basis. 'A very useful book . . . a valuable addition to any careers library – well written clear and interesting.' *Phoenix/ Association of Graduate Careers Advisory Services.* 'I learned a lot from the book and was impressed at the amount of information that it contained.' *Newscheck/Careers Service Bulletin.* Mark Hempshell is a freelance writer who specialises on overseas employment topics.

208pp illus. 1 85703 177 6. 3rd edition.

HOW TO FIND TEMPORARY WORK ABROAD
A world of opportunities for everyone

Nick Vandome

Would you like the chance to work abroad – perhaps to expand your horizons, finance an extended holiday, or use some 'time between'? Whatever your aims and interests, this practical book has something for you. It explains where to find the opportunities suited to your own particular interests, how to apply and be selected, how to manage money, passports, permits, insurance and accommodation, and how to get the most out of your experience overseas. Whether you plan to stay abroad for a couple of weeks or most of the year, this is the book for you, packed with valuable employment advice and contacts. Nick Vandome is a young freelance writer who has spent a year abroad on three occasions, in France, Australia, Africa and Asia. His articles have appeared in *The Guardian, The Scotsman, The Daily Telegraph* and elsewhere. He is also author of *How to Get a Job in Australia* in this series.

160pp illus. 1 85703 109 1.

GOING TO UNIVERSITY
How to prepare yourself for all aspects of student life

Dennis Farrington

Are you an A-Level student? Are you planning to apply for a place at university? 'Going to university' is something which over 300,000 people do each year, committing several years of their lives and a fair amount of money in the process. If you are planning to join them, this book is a guide through the increasingly complex maze of choices in higher education. It will show you how to get the best from the system, how to choose what is most appropriate, how to satisfy yourself about quality, how to decide where to live, how to get good advice about a career, and many other topics. Follow the expert advice in this book, and make sure you make the right choices at this important stage of your career. You may not get a second chance. Dr Dennis Farrington has worked in senior positions in university administration since 1981. He is a leading authority on the institution-student relationship and the way universities work.

128pp illus. 1 85703 405 8.